… bipolar passages …

jon langione

PublishAmerica
Baltimore

Hardcover 978-1-4560-0738-6
Softcover 978-1-4560-0739-3
PUBLISHED BY PUBLISHAMERICA, LLLP
www.publishamerica.com
Baltimore

Printed in the United States of America

to cathey langione

other books by jon and cathey langione
canzio: a sal luca gig
santa is out there, christmas tales from the edge: a sal luca gig
genesis encryption: a sal luca gig

acknowledgements

my loving wife cathey has worked long hours editing bipolar passages ... for catheys care of my written word ... i am deeply indebted ... bipolar passages could not have been written without her

as for sal luca ... well i just made him up

... sal ...

... it was a dark and stormy night ... i always wanted to start a book with that ... surprises come to you and you have to be ready for them ... an opportunity in the form of a manuscript came to me one night as i walked in from the jetway and settled into my seat ... perhaps the surprise sought me out in some metaphysical fashion ... from the hand of the author to me ...i was on a flight from philadelphia to new york city ... for an interview on bob kaal s morning talk show ... i was on the midnight redeye ... a bulge in the seat pocket in front of me caught my attention ... i pulled it open and a thick pack of papers was exposed ... it was about a half a ream of paper in a flimsy binder ...

... i pulled it out and leafed through it ... it appeared to be a book manuscript draft or a thesis ... it was titled ... bipolar passages by jon langione ... i doubt he intended to leave it on the plane ... at first i thought of turning it over to the flight attendant but decided against it ... i could see the book being passed from hand to hand until it was thrown into the circular file ... plus ... finding this guy would be a challenge ... it was not as if it was critical to him ... i was sure he had it on his computer ...

... i decided to read it ... what the hey ... i had the time ... the book was written in all lower case and with ellipses allowing the reader to follow along with the writers stream of thought ... this is the first manuscript i have seen written in a modern texting format ... bipolar passages is a learning experience for those with bipolar ... but i am getting ahead of myself ...

... i read half the book on the flight to nyc and finished it on the way back to philly ... after returning i started the task of finding jon

... being italian i knew the name was uncommon ... what i did in alphabetical order was click state by state on to phone directories ... i soon got lucky ... i came upon his name in arizona ... at least it was not wyoming ...

... jon was elated when i called him ... although he did have the manuscript backed up on the computer ... he appreciated me looking him up and calling ... he asked if i read it ... not only did i tell him i read it ... i thought it was a page turner ... i told him it was a good candidate for publication ... he was surprised when i told him that ... jon thought the book may be too intimate to interest a broad based readership ... he did not know if mental health topics sold well or if publishers would even take a look at it ...

... i told him the intimacy of the book is what made it so readable ... so engrossing ... i told him i could help him with the publication as i was in the business of writing ... he was delighted to have my assistance and asked me to proceed ... he offered a percent of the sales ... i told him it was on the house ...

... bipolar passages is an enlightening ... sympathetic ... and often a funny reach into the world of the bipolar ... i asked jon if i could interview him as to the stages of his life and his illness ... he replied that not only could i interview him ... he wants me to include the interview in the book ... i said it was a deal ... as we moved along through his life i came to realize that jon was presenting the material in the mind set at each stage ... the book matures as jon does ... each age of the story ... unique ...

... i wrote this introduction in the same format as the book ... my name is sal luca and i am a reporter with the philadelphia daily editor ...

... broken broker ...

... next to the word stress in the dictionary is a photo of a stockbroker ... that is what i was on that bleak winter day in florida ... the city is not important ... i was just a cog in the wheel of a big operation that spent the day cold calling strangers and asking them to send in large amounts of money to invest in small cap stocks ... the firm i was with brought small companies ... about two hundred million in assets ... public ... the whole effort was based on commissions ... the commissions were at five percent ... hey ... you get a million dollar client ... the firm gets fifty thousand ... and i got about ten thousand ... i never had a million dollar client ...

... stock broking is like the two dollar window at the race track ... it is what keeps the track open ... and what kept my firm open was the day to day grind to turn out iras for a couple of grand ... each two grand ira paid the firm a hundred bucks ... ad it up ... it takes a lot of those sales to even make twenty four thousand a year ... of course i hit a good lick every once in awhile ... i guess i was pulling in about thirty thousand a year ...

... not bad ... really ... not too bad at all for just starting out ... but just think of the grind ... i prided myself for making three hundred calls a day ... a lot of the other brokers had a line about five paragraphs long ... like ...hi my name is fred farquard and i am with the buglump brokerage firm ... now is the time to make some really smart moves in a very aggressive market ... what a line of bandini and can you imagine saying that three hundred times a day ...

… i used to say … hi my mane is jon langione … i am a stock broker … may i send you my card … and then i would shut up and let them talk … the first response was …

… how did you get my number …

… you are on my list of investors …

… how did i get on that …

… have you invested in the past with the buglump firm … my firm … we are a leading firm in high tech small cap stocks … how about picking up a quarter block of stock …

… how much is that jon …

… two hundred twenty thousand dollars …

… are you nuts …

… yes i am nuts … crazy enough to tell you right now is the time to get in the market with everything you have …

… heck … i do not have much …

… how much can you go …

… oh … maybe two thousand …

… okay … go with two grand on melminex industries …

… what do they do …

… they make conibline pins and cospin rods …

… okay i guess i can go with two thousand … jon … can we put this in a ira …

… sure … and with that the firm just made a hundred bucks … i had to do that three times a day to clear five hundred a week … so when you see those business channel cutaways to the brokerage house floors with all the phone chatter and five computer screens to manage … well … they all are not making that much money … but they look like it …

… i did the suspenders thing … crisp shirt … power tie … you do better in the business when you dress the part … it sounds odd to dress to make phone calls … but i also met clients in the office … we had a strange array of investments … from electronics to silos … we hawked the wares and the opportunity to make a buck …

… it did not dawn on me until years later … when cathey and i wrote an investment column just how whacko the whole business is

… investing is nothing but using your hard earned money and taking a chance with your future …

… how could i convince people to put enough faith in me to invest their future … well … that was the stress … not the sales … not the making commissions … it was making enough calls to get enough clients … thet was the worry …

… was i right … was it a good investment on behalf of the folks trusting me … the stress came with the fear of them losing their money … i had once invested in the market and got churned and burned as the saying goes … i had no desire to get back in the market with anything but mutual funds … it dawned on me that i should put my advice where my money was … and thus i started recommending mutuals … but no matter what i did it was all falling apart … i was falling apart and i could not figure out what was wrong … but not everything was wrong . that meant i myself was wrong …

… when you start to concentrate on yourself and have the added dilemma of trying to cope with everything around you going nutzy … my mind concentrated on nothing but me … if i could just figure me out i could then figure it all out … i thought i had the capacity to do that … if everyone around me would just understand … little did i know that i was on a different frequency … and i could not fine tune my life …

… i used to go into the firm at seven … be ready for the market at nine thirty and after the market would close at four i would research old accounts and try to gin up business with them … then i would go home about seven and tune into the business channels … this would last to eleven and then to bed for fitful sleep … i was burning myself out … but not in a business sense … i was burning out the psyche … i was becoming a brain basket case …

… then one day the whole thing crashed about ten in the morning … i passed my first wife on the way out the door … she was going to the same firm where she worked in the pit … the administration of the firm …

… i threw my clothes on the floor and crawled into the bed in the extra room … i just pulled the covers over my head and tried to block it all out … i stayed there for hours and then i had a lucid moment … a moment of clarity as the psyche saying goes … i called a one eight hundred number in the yellow pages under mental health or some such category …

… it was a clinic in california … the staff called back with a plane ticket number … i am jumping ahead … when they found out i had insurance from uncle sam i was admitted in a flash … so they called back with the ticket information and off i went … i parked the car in the airport lot and wrote down the lot and space number … when i got into the terminal i called home and left a message on the answering machine … threw my carryon bag stuffed with two days clothes and got on the plane … when i arrived i was picked up by a limo and whisked to the clinic … the pamphlet in the front lobby read a place for healing … heal what … was my question … what was wrong with me …

… *what did you think was wrong with you … tell me what you thought you had …*

… i did not feel as if something … say an illness was wrong with me … i felt as though i was wrong … plus i was adverse to being labeled mentally ill … i considered that an aberration not an illness …

… *how did your family react to you …*

… it was just my wife and me … she was worn out by then … i had been … well … there was something wrong with me for quite some time … i felt bad for the situation that she was in … seeing me like i was … our daughter was living in texas at the time … but she knew something was up and like her mother knew for a very long time …

… *is this the first time you sought help …*

… kind of …

... when it all started ...

... quaint was the word for our little town ... we lived north of the town of quaint on a farm ... there were fields of corn and potatoes ... of course the name of the town was not quaint but for the sake of the history let s call it that ...

... a couple of kids were at the house down the road ... i had played with them before ... unless they showed up i went for months without someone to play with ... i was on a farm with the adults ... all i knew was the adults and their behavior ...

... i was about five ... back then a five year old could walk all over the place and not fear kidnapping or abuse by some guy in a car ... it was just me and the farm the animals and sometimes the visiting kids ...

... one time when the kids and i played out in the field near my house ... we got to rough housing and my shirt got torn ... we were not fighting ... just rolling around and chasing each other ...

... as soon as i saw the torn shirt i knew i was going to get beat ... i got angry at the kids for causing me to tear the shirt ... my anger exploded into a tantrum ...

... there was a small wooden bridge from the house across a creek to the farm road ... i stood on the bridge ... the kids and their parents were watching me as i screamed and jumped up and down ... tears were running down my cheeks ... i yelled and yelled ... completely incoherent i began to tear the shirt off my body ... i turned and ran away to my house ... i was scared to death about what was about to happen and it did ...

… my parents did not wonder how my shirt got torn or if i was hurt … or if i was all right … no … their system of parenting … whack him on the butt first … then sort things out …

… i was completely out of control … my parents called it grandfathers bucking up … my grandfather used to rage and from that i learned to do the same … all i was doing was following the behavior i saw … my mother would rage and my step-father would put up with it … my grandfather would rage and my grandmother would put up with it …

… my uncle … my mothers brother would often ask what trouble did i get into or what the hell was wrong with me … he would grab me by the collar and kick me on the butt … my little butt took a lot of abuse back then … i was never beat to bruising or any scars but i got hit so often i lived in fear of messing up …

… came the time when i had to test for school … i was going into the first grade and had to take some kind of skills test … i got them all correct … and because my grandmother was a former school teacher i was able to read a bit … i had been accepted into the first grade … eight hours a day … from the bus trip to and from and the time in school i would be away from the house … i got to be with other kids …

… the realization hit me … and it did not take long … that i did not fit in … from my first day of school … it was not challenging … not that i was bored … i was only interested in getting the work done to move on to other things …

… there were two first grade classes … the teacher i got was meaner than a snake … however we were more disciplined than the other class … in all things we towed the line … i was afraid of her but she never laid a hand on me … the only time i got paddled was in the second grade and it was for talking … i was stand-offish but i was talkative …

… my forte was reading … and because i read so well i was able to get ahead of the learning curve with everything … i think it was during the summer break between the second and third grade that my parents bought encyclopedias and with them came a set of children s books ... ah ... a break from the rough treatment of the butt ... that first summer break ... rather than go out to play by myself ... i would sit for hours reading ... i ended up having to go to the doctors as my parents thought i was ill ... they took me to see the doctor to see if it was a mental thing ... since i had a complete reversal in my behavior ... i had settled down to an odd being to them ... i was quiet ... i would sit on the couch for hours ... even though my parents no longer had to bother with me ... i still felt like a bother ... i sensed i was always bothering them ...

... i did not know what to tell the doctor ... i think he diagnosed me as someone who likes to read ... it was not an aberrant condition according to him ...

... hoping that my parents no longer saw me as a bother ... i was given a boston terrier as a christmas present ... i was quite young and of course was not responsible enough to take care of a dog ... he was a delight to me ... i had someone to play with ... and being on the farm we could go anywhere ... i loved buster ... buster loved me ...

... until buster came along all my friends were imaginary ... kids without playmates often develop an unsual imagination ... or maybe i had a talent for making things up ... i made up friends and played well with them ... no arguments with fake friends ...

... and i was not deprived ... i had all the toys one can wish for ... but buying a bow and arrow set for an eight year old was not such a good idea ... i did grow up in an environment of shooting animals ... hunting was the big deal and i wanted to keep up with the adults ... buster and i hunted the hills around the farm ...

... i shoot an arrow at the paperboy as my parents were upset with him ... seems the paper was twenty four cents a week ... they would set a quarter out for him and he would not leave the penny in change ... they railed against the slight ... the bilking of a cent ... so too i continued their behavior of anger against the paperboy ... i shot at him with an arrow ... he never told my parents and i had to face him at the school bus stop ... he did not beat me up ... i figured he was a better person than i was ... he talked to me as if it never happened ... but after that he left the penny ... i think that was my first lesson of the use of force to gain a satisfactory outcome … i did not think of it that way but as i look back on it i do now …

… most of my childhood i flipped fits for no reason at all … but also i did so to get my own way … but that tactic seldom worked … the butt would be warmed again …

… were you just … well … you were just mirroring what you had experienced in the home … would you call it raging … is that really a good name for it …

… maybe raging is too strong a word for me at that stage of my childhood …

… of course i could not have deciphered my condition at that age … i recall it though … i recall it very vividly …

… you seem to be dwelling on the bad parts … was your life that rough …

… what i am doing is trying to frame the experiences and the thought processes i had at the time … i do remember at this age i lived in a lot of fear of being condemned … i lived in fear of messing up …

… you were so young and you recognized that …

… condemnation will come up a lot … you know from reading the manuscript …

… fear of condemnation … you were only ten …

… yeah … nine or ten …

… do you think other bipolars reading this will relate …

… absolutely …

… i am only going to delve into the bipolar … if that is all right …

… absolutely …

... still too young to know ...

... between the fourth and fifth grade we moved into a small town on the susquehanna river ... it was now a different set of rules ... here i also came to realize that i was not on the same wave length as the rest of the kids ... i still stood off from the crowd ... the primary reason for this was i was bad at sports ... no i was really terrible ... on the farm ... alone ... i had no experience with the games kids played ... it is hard to play pitch and catch by yourself ... i grew up indifferent to sports ... the other reason i did not fit in ... i was italian and stood out as i had a lot of vowels in my name ... my father left when i was about three months old ... save that for later ...

... in essence i was a minority ... all the other kids i went to school with were german ... there were no blacks ... they were not allowed to buy property in the town ... one family of blacks lived in a house for servants ... the other black person in town was a grave digger who lived in a shack ... i was estranged from blacks ... i had never seen them except in the city nearby ... growing up ... i noticed blacks were not allowed to eat in restaurants ... essentially blacks were not allowed ... my parents disliked them and therefore so did i ... for no reason at all ... all the time in school i was the minority ... i soon learned and i felt the parents of the kids really did not want me around ... and they thought me to be a weird kid ... i was weird in the sense that i lived life like i was always in a movie ... my life took on the fantasy of being a movie star ... it came from my imagination and growing up with tv ...

... when i was eight my parents bought a tv ... it was a round screen about ten inches in diameter ... i remember the first show i saw on it … it was about the fall of dien bien phu … i had no idea where that was or what it was about … i just fell in love with the idea that i could escape into the tube …

… later while living in the small town i would be left alone at night while my mother worked in a restaurant and my step father stayed out in the evenings … i had the tv and it was through that that i became a night person … i could not wait until friday night when i could stay up and watch the late show and the late late show … old movies … half of them adventure films … i especially liked war movies … i thought soldiers in war were the ultimate … of course not in a real war … a movie war … i saw killing to be just for movies …

… an event in my life sticks with me and will as long as am alive … i still feel dreadful about it … a young bird fell out of a nest and i thought it would probably die … i wanted to give it a decent burial but it was not yet dead … i poured gas on it and lit it on fire … of course it screeched and flapped around … i was shocked when it did this … i then buried it in a shoe box with a cross over the grave … it was a horrible thing to do and this is the first time i have admitted it to anyone … oh i have mentioned that i killed birds with my bb gun … but i never told anyone about this … i carry the shame of this with me and time and time again ask for forgiveness from that poor tortured little bird … i have been told that killing birds with a bb gun is just part of a boys growing up … i do not buy it … it was the sign of a disturbed kid … i was that kid and i think it saved the lives of animals to follow … when i was twelve my grandfather took me hunting and i remember shooting three rabbits … one was so close to me i could see the terror in its eyes … dreadful … i went hunting after that … i shot at animals but purposely missed them … i could not kill them anymore … i was ridiculed for being such a bad shot … i hated guns … i was not in step with the men in the family … i did not like hunting …

… i went along deer hunting with no intentions of killing bambi … i had a wool hunting outfit and would sit for hours on a deer stand … one day sitting leaning against a tree i dozed of … i felt a rough touch on my face … i looked up to see two doe standing in front of me …

one had licked me on the face … that did it … i never even bothered to hunt again …

… but my aversion to hunting was not the only thing that distanced me from the family … i was disowned for smoking … hey … i was twelve … what twelve year old kid is not going to try something like that … big deal … but not in my household … i was considered so bad that my mother took me to her parents place … when she dropped me off she told them she was disowning me … being disowned like that i figured i was getting in the way of her drinking …

… by this time a had a brother ten years my junior … my step father would spend his time with what was now his own kid and they would be gone most evenings … good … it left me alone with the tv and my movies … i was even staying up late on school nights … becoming more of a night person …

… growing up i was told time and again by my mother that i interrupted her life … if she would not have had me her life would have been much more successful … i was into my teens when i realized that line of bandini … bandini being a brand of fertilizer … that line of bandini did not float … she was twenty three when she had me … by then she could have had a masters … but at twelve the drinking my parents were doing was becoming obvious to me … i did not realize though that it was beyond normal to have a distributer truck show up and unload cases of beer every week … most households would get a six pack or so … but cases … although i did not realize the specifics of it … the drinking took over their lives … especially my mother …

… even with the home environment of an alcoholic family i did well in school … even though it bored me to tears … i wanted to run away and be in the movies … if i seem to be dwelling on this … it is because i thought that actors were somebody … i thought of myself as a nobody and it was reinforced by the very nature of the household in which i lived …

… i will give you some examples … i dropped a water bottle one time and for that my mother smacked me across the face … another time i said ah nuts and my step father hit me in the mouth and broke off a tooth … like the book reading when i was younger … i settled down and withdrew again … i just stayed in my room or sat out in my pigeon coop and talked to the birds … i had no friends come around … i had very little outside activities … i was just happy to stay at home … stay at home in my solitude … which was easy as my parents were not there most of the time … i have very few good memories of my childhood …

… then i moved into the seventh grade … the studies were quite different from grade school and a bit more challenging … that is until i got a handle on the work and coasted again … but something was missing … somehow there was a hole in my psyche … it went beyond being different …

… one day while watching activity on the playground … i did not participate as … well … after awhile it was tiring to be last in choosies … well … this older kid walks up to me and started talking to me … i was surprised by his interest in me … we talked for awhile and then headed to his place to play pool … he had a pool table … he was my first true friend … he was three years older than me but we hit it off … i guess he saw a maturity in me … and we had similar backgrounds … we had good taste in clothes and had dysfunctional families …. kids of a feather so to say … plus he was good looking and had a lot of girls interested in him … i was interested in girls since the first grade when i went home and told my aunt that a girl in my class was pretty neat … i was always comfortable in the company of girls …

… i was developing into a radical with my thought processes … i would say my illness started to raise its head then … i was about thirteen … i loved the adventures my new friend and i had … we would crawl under the bridge crossing the susquehanna … a dangerous sort of stunt … but it was fun to me … danger became a part of my life at that age … this too was a part of the development of the illness … mania had obviously set in …

… my desire to be alone before i met my friend was depression … and the off the wall things we did were mania on my part … when my friend was old enough to get a car … we loved that old pontiac … we kept it so clean … so shined up we waxed the paint off it and rubbed it down to the primer … he taught me to drive a standard transmission

… he would let me … at only fourteen … drive and swing by girls homes to show off … this gave them the impression that i was older than i was … when i was old enough to legally drive i remember the one and oly time my mother took me out for a driving lesson … as she was telling me how to drive a stick i pulled right out … she was speechless …

… my friend and i hung for two years until he finished high school and i moved into the city as a result of my mothers divorce … he went into the air force and i only saw him a few times after that …it gave me the idea that i might try the service … it was a seed planted in my mind … it would prove to be a great opportunity …

… i liked the city and i was living in an apartment in my aunts place … my mother and her sister never got along … i thought my aunt was cool … she seemed to be in control of everything … she also had a boyfriend that was beyond cool … he was a former semi-pro football player and hung out with me quite a lot …

… junior high in the big city was quite an experience … it was my first exposure to black people … coloreds as the family called them … civil rights movements had not come to the streets yet … there was a divide between the races … i started to get in a lot of fights … there were no gangs but there were a lot of cliques … of which i fit into none … my last year in junior high i went out for football … a very bad decision … i was short and skinny … on end sweeps the back field would run over me … that experience taught me that it was just another thing i was no good at … my school work started to suffer for it … it turned me off of sports even more … i was wrong to think i could learn football … i was taught very little but i did learn that if i could not play i would not get to play … i was on the sidelines the whole season … i did get a letter for it … but so did everyone else on the team … it gave me the idea that anything that came my way was of no value if it was given to me … what value was i … i had no self esteem … more evidence of my illness encroaching … i cannot stand the term low self esteem … i think it is psycho babble … although i did not know it then … for just about the whole ninth grade … i was in a deep depression …

… i was not even in senior high school and sent to a psychiatrist … what brought it on was that i was acting out scenes from tv shows … the teachers thought i was out of control … i thought it was cool that i remembered the lines after hearing them only one time … but my memory was to serve me well in the future …

… i had another summer of being by myself and sitting in my pigeon coop … also i came to figure out that my aunt who was in control was in control because she was a control freak … she also had a habit of following a compliment by a put down … i adjusted to it …

… by this time in my life i was completely in my head … by that i mean i was grading myself all the time … because i had become a weird kid i was always being picked on … my cool uncle told me a secret … when a bully picks on you … just smack … it worked … even though i was so skinny i had no force behind my swings … after awhile i was left alone … the bullies were just a pack of loud mouths … i withdrew more and more …

… my aunt had a beauty shop on the property … i liked to hang out there … now to be fair … my aunt did a lot for me … clothes and money and things a boy my age would be interested in … but it was her insults that impacted me the most … to get the goodies i had to suffer the bummed out conversations … i once told her i thought it was cool to be italian … wrong thing to say … i got a lengthy lecture on how bad it was to be italian … no wonder i was depressed …

… my life was not horrible by any stretch of the imagination … what i am pointing out is the mounting illness … the thought processes … the depression and the mania … the condition of my mind and the behavior that would put people off … i garnered a lot of strange looks as i got older … i was truly a weird kid and i could not figure out why so many adults had to bad mouth me to my face …

… the last day of the ninth grade when we got our final report cards the homeroom teacher found it in himself to point out that i had done so lousy in everything … i thought it was a little unfair … it hurt … i had all a s and b s … how could i have done so badly … but i had experienced this before when the football coaches would point out to the other players how lousy i was ... i put that off to the stupidity of the coaches ...

... i was glad to be out of the ninth grade ... it was another indication of my illness ... always relieved to be getting away from something ... the move from the small town to the city ... getting away from the family life in which i was so unhappy ... so depressed ... each place i went i would have to force myself on others ... i cannot remember but one incidence of anyone coming to my house to get me to come out and play ... it was always that i would force myself on the group ... i tired of that and found a way out ...

... i went to beauty school ... hey ... it was stacked to the ceiling with girls ... i did not realize that being straight was an exception to the rule of male hairdressers ... it was a follow on to the one thing i was good at in junior high and that was being in plays and being the mc for assemblies ... somehow i fell into that ... it was cool standing up before all those people and not being nervous ... it brought on a short period of mania each time i would do it ... the action brought on the mania ... not the mania getting me involved in the act of performing ... i did not realize it but i was controlling my mania ... but then i would slip back into depression ...

... there came a point when i was taken to the doctor to figure out what was wrong with me ... again ... but my mother could not articulate the actions that lead her to bring me there ... all she knew was that something was wrong with me ... wrong became the mantra of the family except my cool uncle ... he liked the fact that i was such a quick wit ... and he was impressed with my stage work and being so quick to get the lines down ... and he told me so ... plus ... i will give my aunt and him credit ... they came to the few activities i was involved in ... my mother never showed up ...

... the older i got the more of a pain in the ass i became ... i was failing the tenth grade ... no matter ... we moved again ... ah ... another fresh start ... i was getting used to my mothers geographic cures ... that is more psycho babble ...

... there is a lot in this chapter ... seems to me you were in a stage of mania for quite awhile ...

… i controlled my mental state by my conduct … it was as if i could put myself in a manic state … i would think up things to do to look forward to … that is telling evidence of bipolar … or at least that is what i have been told …

… what is … i missed something …

… i have been told that evidence of bipolar is always having something to look forward to …

… but you seemed to have done so well until the tenth grade … what was up … boredom …

… not really … i just found it easy … school work was not all that hard … i was just not interested …

... ah ... mania ...

... life was about to get real interesting ... the rage side of mania was about to raise its head ... we returned to the home of my grandparents ... no longer were they on the farm but moved into the small town south of the farm ... the reason we moved there is that my mother was just falling apart ... i have no other way to put it ...

... i was six feet tall and skinny ... and i had developed an intimidating personality thanks to living in the city ... i owe a debt of gratitude to those punks i had to deal with in the city ... now in a farming community high school i was considered a city kid ... who are you the football player ... i did not tell them i sucked ... of course i was made fun of for going to beauty school at night ... i was also about to go from disinterest to contempt for the whole school thing ... school seemed to be getting in my way ... of what ... i did not know ...

... i picked up my grades coasting in the classes ... i had some choice of classes and i took the easy ones ... i excelled in english and avoided math ... i liked the english as i could just make up stories and get a good grade for the effort ... it was my imagination that pulled me through ... i did not like the structure of the math classes so i did not sign up for one ... this should have been caught by the school staff ...

... the first fourteen years of my life i lived in seven different places ... it was from pillar to post ... it may sound as if i had a terrible childhood ... i did ... i raised myself which i came to understand in a alcoholic family is typical of the eldest child ... by the time i moved with my mother into my grandparents house my little brother was gone with my step father … and my mother seemed to be none the worse for it …

… getting in the way of drinking is a heavy responsibility for a fourteen year old …and just like an alcoholic i started to develop resentments … and i carried these to my school life … fighting became my way of acting out … i do not ever remember winning one … i was just angry all the time …

… there were three times during my stay at my grandparents that i should have been taken to see a physician … get this … i was in the dining room while my grandparents were in the living room and for no reason at all i passed out and fell to the floor … my head bounced off the floor … they did not even get up … the question was … what is going on with you … now the context of this is that i had just done something wrong and fell to the floor … if my daughter fell down like that i would take her to see a doctor … but i was too much trouble for them … why bother … that incident was not the only time i felt dizzy … i never found out what caused it … never had a chance to … anytime i was hurt i was plagued by the same question … what did you do … what is wrong with you … you hear that often enough and you begin to feel there is something wrong … but i felt i beat them to the punch … i knew something was wrong with me early in my teens … my family just confirmed it …

… i got knocked out … i was hanging out at a service station by a pool hall and one of the guys went to punch me on the arm like boys do … instead he hit me right on the button … right on the chin and knocked me out … he just cold cocked me and again i hit the floor … only this time the floor was cement and i really bounced my head … i had to be helped home … i lived about a half block away … somehow i got into bed and did not wake up until about seven in the evening … i went downstairs to find my grandparents and uncle there … they saw the bruise on my chin and instead of asking what happened … i was asked what i had done to get those bruises … blamed again for something … what that something was i was blamed for i never found out … but it had to be my fault … i could have had a concussion …

but that thought apparently never crossed their minds … again they did not take me to a doctor … again too much of a bother …

… the third time was real neglect … i was to meet this kid across town at another pool hall for a fight … i told my folks about it … and my grandfather told me he would drive me over there … now … as i consider this in context … he was sending a skinny kid that had no ability to fight in harms way to fight not one but three … as it turned out i did not get past the first one … get this … my relatives were always telling me to get into fights … as i reflect upon this insanity … they were living out their violence through me …

… so … i end up with this kid on my back on the ground … and he hits me along the side of my head … my left eye went blank and my cheek and temple felt crushed … i was bruised along the entire side of my face … although i got my site back … my head was reeling and my sight was blurry for a few days … the hurtful … hateful thing my grandfather said to me sticks in my mind to this day … he said … boy you just cannot fight … he laughed and he shook his head … again i was not taken to the doctor … i spent the rest of my high school days hating and embarrassed by the experience and wanting to get away … the damage to my face left me open to ridicule … i was ashamed of my performance … of course my uncles and everyone else in the family told me what a loser i was … up until then i stayed angry … but now i had internal rage that kept me in a manic state for months … of course i was depressed over this … i was constantly being egged on to get into fights by my family … then told i was no good at it …

… three times my head had been beaten around and no help was sought … had i been seen by a doctor for the injuries it might have lead to my being diagnosed with something … but doubtful bipolar or manic depression …back then these were relatively unknown diagnoses to many in the healing profession …

… one thing i did realize and that was i was living in stink … i did not realize at the time it was alcoholic stink … but it was dysfunctional stink … my mother was completely out of control … she worked in the booze business and was constantly drinking and the boyfriends … good grief … drunks of course …

… an odd sidelight to all of this is that no one ever took my picture … sounds strange to think about that … as i am writing i realize i have no photos of my teen years … i could have been a great spy as i did not exist … i was an unperson … no history … at this time in my life i came to the conclusion i could not do anything … i was becoming a failing mess in high school … could not play sports and had no friends … oh i had some i could hang out with … but it was as if i was forcing myself on them … they never sought me out … i could not invite anyone to the house as i had no room of my own to take them to … i slept on a single bed in my grandfathers room … i had a small closet … i did bring some people over to the house for about ten minutes when no one was home … i felt both guilty and afraid that i would be caught …

… now this is insanity … get this … i went up into the attic to get some fishing stuff and my uncle came into the house … he yelled at me for being up there …grabbed me by the scruff of the neck and kicked me in the butt … that was a confusing one … i lived there and the tackle was mine … that was the closest i came to running off during my childhood … i had visions of going to new york city and doing what … i had no idea … i hated myself for not running away … so … one more example that i did not have the guts to do something … i believe the thoughts of running away turned into hallucinations … when i thought about it even though i did not go i became elevated in my mood … it was my little secret that i was running away to new york city in my imagination … it made me laugh at the other kids … they held me up to ridicule that i was from the city near our farm town … what if i was from the biggest city of them all … my thoughts were focused on the run away kid that i was too scared to be … hey … dreams are dreams … this threw me into a very expansive mood … irritable over the fights and the ridicule … elevated moods over the day dreaming about being in new york city … and … expansive in my personality … these are all symptoms of stages of bipolar in adolescents …

… during this stage i recalled the time i was taken to see a tv cowboy star at an arena … the only memories i had of the event was after going there i would lie in my bed hoping he would come and take me away to be with him on his big ranch … i spent a lot of time in my head trying to figure out ways to get away …

… all my illusions were grandiose … i cannot remember a time when my thinking was less than the impossible for a farm kid in a little town in pennsylvania … movie star … on a big ranch … beating up every one of my enemies … grandiose illusions are another symptom of bipolar … i became more and more withdrawn … more and more reclusive … more and more into the tv … … at fifteen i was a pack a day smoker … straights … no filters for me … my mother bought me my cigarettes … i would sit in front of the tv and smoke … the tv gave me pleasure and so did the nicotine …

… i guess i bugged the family when i was with them … my racing thoughts would keep me talking and running on at the mouth … racing speech or excessive talkativeness is another trait of a manic depressive … all this adds up as i look back …

… thoughts would stay with me for days … i would sit in class in school and just think of the possibilities for my life … however … i was on track to be a dropout and a low wage earner … i did not realize what i was doing to myself and my family did not care … i used to sign the report cards myself so as not to get the condemnation for the low grades … they did not care about the grades … they just used the report cards as another way to tell me there was something wrong with me …

… i could live with the condemnation … i was living with it … just watch the tube and stay out of the way … never did the school call to say that i was a problem … neither did a school ever call to tell anyone in my family that i was failing … as silly as it may sound i believe i was considered a minority in the school … and who cares about some minority kid … plus the teachers knew i was related to the langiones in the city … with the exception of my one uncle on the italian side the rest of the langiones had not a thing to do with me … it seems when you are dumped on the doorstep as a three month old kid the resentment carries to the kid …

… my last year of school was just my showing up … woody allen said ninety percent of anything is showing up … well i disregarded the other ten percent … the only classes i enjoyed were english and art … it was because of the english class that i decided to leave high school behind as soon as i was seventeen … here is the reason … arriving at the school the first day of my junior year i was given my schedule … english was not going to be much of a challenge as i read a lot … in the first class of the first day i received an assignment that showed no imagination … the assignment was … write a paper on what i did on my summer vacation … how original … all i did was hang around the town … not being very good at sports i joined then quit the ball team … i did get half decent at pool … but that is merely a sign of a misspent youth … so … this is what i did … i wrote a paper about how … as i was walking home the last day of school of the previous year i was captured by gypsies and taken to the wilds of canada … soon i became part of the gypsy band and traveled with them … i learned their customs and dances and a bit of romanian … but … i knew i had to get back home to go to school … so i escaped and made my way back from canada through the mountains of pennsylvania … i lived off of nuts and berries … when i finally made it home form this adventure … my clothes were in rags and that is why … on the first day of school … i had on new clothes … duh … everyone had new clothes on the first day of school … i learned a big lesson from this story … two really … the first one was if all else fails … make something up … as i did with the gypsy story and my reward was an a plus grade … the second lesson was much different … it seems the english teacher gave the story to the assistant principal to read as it was the highlight of the stories … the guy calls me in his office … throws the story down on his desk and says … this is a lie … i saw you around town all summer …

… it was difficult not to laugh … i just shrugged my shoulders … how could i answer something like that … but that moment … that insanity … that one stupid event brought on by an adult that lacked basic common sense was to change my life … it was a moment of clarity for me … at that very moment … that very tiny particle of time … the clock stood still for a nanosecond … in that tiny sweep of the second hand i decided that i would do everything i could to be gone from all this … all this craziness … the whole time i thought i was crazy … this day … this moment … that was not the case … all i had to do was get through this one year until the twenty sixth of june nineteen sixty three … my seventeenth birthday …

… from that day forward my free thinking would connive a way to get on the way … to kick my own butt down the street …

… watch what happens … it dawned on me that i owed no one … that thesis by the family that i owed them no longer held true … i was now searching for a way out … telling me i owed them for providing for me was more boozed up resentful thinking … but what is a sixteen year old supposed to make of it … owe them for what … owe them what … i could not do anything … i was about to be a high school dropout … then … ah … another then … then came that fateful day in march of sixty three when my step father was visiting my grandparents … seems he ran into a navy recruiter … the recruiter gave him his card … so my step father gives me the card and tells me to look him up when i graduate … that would have been at least fifteen months away and it was not going to happen … so why give me the card … who knows … it sparked an idea in my head … i made an appointment to see the recruiter …

… i skipped school and went to see the navy guy … we had an appointment in the recruiting office in the city post office … two oclock came and went and no navy guy … the army recruiter came out and asked if he could help me … i said that i was waiting for the navy guy … i sat there another half hour and still no navy … so the army guy comes out again … hey … ya want a coke … sure i said … and i stepped into his office …

… i let him know i was only sixteen but was sure my mother would sign for me when i turned seventeen … he did not bat an eye … we can take care of that he said … i was conniving enough to find a way to get the paperwork signed …

… he gave me a forty eight question test … i missed one question … he seemed impressed …

... the next day at school the assistant principal asked me where i had been ... i told him i went to see a recruiter and as soon as i was seventeen i was enlisting ... he shook his head .... laughed .... and walked away ...

... about a week later i took another day off and went to take tests and a physical ... having passed those i was told to call another recruiters office ... what would you like to do was the question ... i replied the army security agency ... the only thing i knew about that organization was that my cousin was in it for three years ... it sounded like something i could do ... being a spy and all ... hey ... what the heck did i know ... the recruiter said all right ... i had to sign a bunch of papers all posted dated to my seventeenth birthday ... i was given a packet of papers to fill out at home ... the papers all had to do with security clearances ... cool ...

... the assistant principal questioned me again as to where i had been ... i told him up at the capitol taking tests for the army ... he laughed again ... i guess he never believed me after the canadian gypsy story ...

... in a week or two i got a call ... all i had to do is bring in my birth certificate with a form signed by my mother with permission for me to join on my seventeenth birthday ... she signed it right away ...

... in the meantime before the school year was ou i got hauled into the guidance counselors office ... it seems that the class was given a test ... a national level test ... for all i know it may have been the s a t ... anyway i got the highest grade on the test for the class ... instead of congratulating me he accused me of cheating ... what was up with that ... i told him i was joining the army on my seventeenth birthday ... he just shook his head ... ya ya ya ...

... on the last day of school for this kid i went around to each class and the teacher gave me a final grade ... i passed everything but chemistry ... when the chemistry teacher put an e on my card he told me how he hated to do it ... i shook his hand ... not to worry i am army bound ... he was the only school staff to believe me ... i took the card home and kept it for some reason ... i had twenty days until i was on my way … just hang out … play pool … smoke cigarettes and watch tv …

… then came the day … i wore a suit coat and tie … it was my birthday and my mother gave me five dollars and a ride to the recruiters office … i was to meet him in the city and he would put me on a bus to the capitol … the army would pick me up at the bus terminal … off i went …

… during my youth i had a laundry list of psyche problems … could not even compete in sports … spent the last three school years being bored … but this adventure … this trip to the armys way of life was the best thing i could have done … what else could i have done … gone to college … huh …

… i am in …

… took a bus from the city to the capitol … from there went to the recruiting station to receive the first of my orders … i was given travel passes for a train ride … then a switch to another bus in trenton …

… but first i was sworn in … it was an oath about defending the country and the constitution … i was officially in the army … another soldier was sworn in with me and as it turned out we would go through basic training together … he was from the farm country … he thought it strange an italian was from a farm … i explained that i was raised by the german side of the family …

… off we went … a van ride to the train station … and then onto my first train ride … i was full of excitement … no turning back now … we ate lunch on the train and gave the waiter our meal vouchers … seems the waiter knew the army system … he told us we could have anything we wanted … anything … what a good way to reflect back on the past few months … here i was being given anything i wanted … the dropping out of school … my mothers signature on the enlistment papers and now what i wanted by complete strangers … it may sound funny but i knew what i wanted as the train chugged on … what i wanted was adventure … adventure was what kept me happy … it was also what kept me in a state of mania …

… it was evening by the time we got into the bus station … we had another voucher for another meal … again the staff at the bus station knew the system … then we were off on the bus to fort dix new jersey … and as it would have it the bus driver also knew the system … it was pitch dark when we arrived … he pulled the bus into a parking lot … and he told us over there … that building where the light is … just report in there ... i was reporting in ... i already felt like a soldier ... we walked over to the building ... a soldier asked us to sign in with our name and rank ... i learned i was a private one ... as low as you can go ... but i was a part of a big machine ... i called the soldier sir ... he told me that was not necessary as he was a private just like us ... he had been there two days and was arranging our incoming to get us transported to our replacement company ... it was then i noticed he was in new fatigues and new boots ...

... there were six or seven of us waiting for transportation ... we were taken in a van to the company barracks and assigned a bunk ... it was about one in the morning ... on the bunk was a stack of bedding ... for my seventeenth birthday i was given a present of two blankets two sheets a pillow and a pillow case ... get some sleep we were told ... we would be getting up at six in the morning ... zero six hundred to be specific ...

... four hours sleep and i was back on my feet ... we were told to line up on some cable out on the company street ... we got some help with the formation as a few reservists were in the barracks ... we were not very good at the formation business but somehow they got us all moved by platoon to a mess hall ... ah ... breakfast ... the food was great ... and that is a compliment to the mess hall ... farm kids eat good ... and so do soldiers ...

... we ate and then lined up again to march to the quartermaster ... we would get our issue of uniforms ... great ...the quartermaster was run by civilians and they took special care to get us uniforms that fit well ... they spent a lot of time with our shoes and boots ... boots have got to fit ... we would be doing a lot of walking ... we went back to the barracks and were told to get changed and that we would have a few hours until we would be going for further tests ... a few of the reservists had shoe polish and i learned the technique of spit shining ...

... the way i felt in that uniform was wonderful ... i was in the army ... i was in uniform ... the whistle blew and we were formed on the cables again ... a sergeant came out and told us we would be circumcised ... i was shocked that i was going to be taken to ... what

… a medical clinic to have the skin cut off my johnson … i became a little anxious … no … i became really anxious … then he told us he was going to cut the extra length off of our belts … i had a twenty eight inch waist … a lot of the belt was tucked into the keepers … he came by each of us and cut the excess off … thus … circumcision … boy was i relieved …

… off we went to lunch and then to a huge classroom with booths … test time … we spent the afternoon in the testing room … one of the tests was the o c test … the officer candidate test … little did i know at the time that my test results on this one would serve me well … we spent about five more days in the replacement depot … the repo depot as it was called … then one morning after breakfast we were told to get our equipment packed … we were going to our basic training company …

… during the week i was in the repo depot i was given the opportunity to call home … my grandfather answered and i told him i was just fine and everything was going along very well … i had been so busy with this and that … but after i talked to my grandfather i reflected how good he was to me and how well he treated me … i also thought about the fight thing … but all things considered i was given good treatment by him … i wanted for nothing … in a moment of unexpected homesickness i considered where i had come from and realized they did the best they could with me and my aberrations … true there was a lot of drinking in the households in which i lived … i hoped they would be proud of me … i told him i was for the first time proud of myself … i think he missed me …

… i thought that arriving at the basic training company would involve a lot of loud sergeants and constant yelling and intimidation … it was nothing like that … we were lined up and our names were read off and we were told to form up in front of our barracks … i was in the third platoon and our platoon leader was a staff sergeant … he again read our names off and he called everyone out and gave them their bunk assignment … everyone that is but me … it seems my name was misspelled … that had plagued me from my first day of school until this very day as i sit here and write … my first reaction was that i was not included … a not belonging trait that has marked me for life … the sergeant told me not to worry … he would get it straightened out … off we went to unpack our gear to be put it in a foot locker and a wall locker … there were pictures on the bulletin board to show us how to line everything up and how to arrange our gear in the foot locker …

… that afternoon we were taken to a line of bleachers and told to take a seat … the company staff introduced themselves … still no yelling at us … this was nothing like the movies at all … i was not disappointed … who wants to be yelled at … as orderly as we conducted ourselves and as organized as the sergeants were … well … there was no reason to yell at us …

… i had rehearsed in my mind the way i would react to the yelling … i was confident i could maintain my composure and not get rattled … i wanted to try it out … no such opportunity … after we received our welcome by the staff we were taught a very brief class in the basics of coming to attention at ease and marching as a platoon … the reservists were put at the front of the formation to help us out …

… there were three strata of soldiers in our company … about one third were regular army … as i was … another third were reserve and national guard … then there were the draftees … many of them were not pleased to be there … the draftees were the older soldiers and much more educated … all had one thing in common … there pay was greatly reduced as compared to their civilian jobs … i caught some ribbing as my enlistment was for four years instead of the normal three … i had to take the extra year as my training would be much longer … i was going into the army security agency and would become a code breaker … the army security agency soldiers were treated a little different … as we were an odd lot … unlike the combat arms of infantry armor and artillery …

… the following day we were marched to a huge gymnasium … we were to receive another briefing by the commanding general … i was really impressed … impressed that a general had any interest in basic training soldiers … he did and had a lot of kind things to say … he also challenged us to do our utmost in our training … i wanted to do that for two reasons … i wanted to do well to stand out but i also did not wish to draw heat …

… as we progressed in our eight weeks of training one adventure after the other came my way … the chemical gas training was especially harrowing … all the classes involved stories of the soldiers in the first world war that got gassed … we were exposed to tear gas and chlorine gas … in the gas chamber we were told to remove our masks and put them back on … when the tear gas hit my eyes i realized how incapacitated i would become under such an attack … we were told to put the masks back on and clear them … at that we were not very successful and each of us had to be lead from the chamber … all of our training was centered around basic infantry tactics … i especially liked the rifle range where i did very well … as we progressed in the training we became more and more confident … i think i was about six weeks into the training when i realized i was going to make it … i had doubts as i always did about finishing things … but this was my chance to prove to myself that i could do something and excel at it … my final basic training grade was ninety nine percent … i was not the same person that showed up at the repo depot … i had accomplished something … for the first time in my life i had graduated … to others in the company it may have been just a matter of going through a program of study and training … but to me … well … it was a new world opened up to me … who needs high school after this … and at no time did it matter that i was a drop out … half the guys from new york city were drop outs and about half the company was from new york city … once on a two day pass i was able to visit the city with a new yorker … we stayed at his uncles place in greenwich village … cool … it was even more cool to have people see me in my uniform and ask how old i was … only seventeen and i am doing as well as the grownups … then i came to realize at seventeen and in the army i was a grownup … even more cool …

… sounds good …

… yeah … but you have got to realize … and i am framing this as to the thoughts i had at that time … joining the army was my reality …

... okay ... so you thought that it was perfectly natural for you to do that ...

… it was … what do you think …

... no ... i think what you did was a real stretch of mania ... i mean it seemed to be the ultimate manic episode ...

… maybe so … but at the time it seemed just fine to me … i mean i took to it and did real well … i had ninety nine on my final …

... it seemed as if you were trying to prove something to someone ... who was it ...

… i guess it was from all the condemnation … i guess i was trying to prove something to other people …

... not yourself ...

… no … not really …

... but were you not self absorbed in the throes of mania ...

… not really … i know i keep saying not really … but it is a little difficult to explain … when i was doing real well in school up until the fourth or fifth grade … after that i was no longer getting a pat on the back for a good report card … but i knew if i got bad grades …

... you would meet with condemnation ...

… yes … really …

... so let us go back a little ... why did you not apply yourself in the tenth and eleventh grade ...

… indifference …

... ah ...

… it did not matter either way … no one cared … it was either indifference or condemnation …

... no pats on the back ...

… until basic training and the sergeants …

... you liked your sergeant ...

… that is because he never put me down …

... no condemnation ...

… he was a real leader … he set the standard for me the rest of my life …

... he had that big of an impact on you ...

… yes … really …

... not the same ...

... i arrived home after basic training ... life was not the same ... i was not the same ... i had matured beyond my years ... a few of the folks around town thought it was foolish of me to quit school and enlist ... i wondered what business it was of theirs ... i had hit upon something i could do and do well ... what did it matter if i went to high school ... looking back on the decision that high school and college right after high school is a lot of hype ... it is over hyped ... i did meet up with some of my former classmates and there was a distance ... it was still summer vacation ... they were going to the twelfth grade and i was going to massachusetts ...

... civilian clothes felt strange as i had worn a uniform for the last ten weeks ... during the two weeks off i reverted to my habit of staying up and watching tv ... had i had more time than those fourteen days i would have fallen into a depression ... for a short time i had nothing to stimulate me ... nothing to look forward to ... i was astute enough to know that i was in the throes of a down period ... i concentrated on the trip to boston ...

... it was the first time i had ever flown ... i was very talkative on the plane ... i was so excited i could barely contain myself ... but that one adventure ... that short plane ride brought me back up ... i flew into boston and then took a bus to fort devens ...

... the building i reported to was more like a campus ... it was a barracks but the building was modern ... i signed in and discovered that we could leave the post evenings and on weekends ... this was new found freedom from the restrictions imposed in basic ... instead of always being on guard and rigid i could relax ... talking to sergeants and officers was normal through the course of the day … the group i was assigned to were all waiting for a class to be formed … this was a new world of fellow soldiers …

… folks think of the army as not having much imagination … it is not true … i was in my element … i did not know the term for it back then but i was with a group of soldiers that thought out of the box … i was the least educated and youngest among them … many had degrees … i was about to enter the world of intelligence … the first course was called basic analysis … we learned communication principles … how messages were administered and the formats in which the messages were sent … the army security agency was an intelligence organization and was subordinated to the national security agency … we were being trained to listen in on other countrys communications … we were opening others electronic mail … this was all fascinating to me … the instructors asked me how old i was … i soon became used to that question … we were taught the military structures of the eastern european countries and russia and china … pretty heady stuff for a teenie bopper … i took to the instruction and really soaked it in …

… there is nothing classified about what i am writing about as these missions have been written about in countless boo by intelligence professionals … no big secrets divulged … sorry … no national security issues … ah … i was about to graduate from a school for the second time … i was on a constant high … constant mania … after basic analysis i was assigned to the radio traffic analysis course … now we were getting to the code breaking …

… winter set in and the ground was covered from november on … we would march to our class rooms into a quadrangle that resembled the old main of many colleges … in fact we were attending instruction that was at the college level … some of my classmates did not make it through the program … i could not think of anything worse than that … what would happen to me if i got bounced out … that thought made me even more determined … we studied codes and how to break them … everything we studied was from morse code or teletype or voice transmissions … we concentrated on the morse and teletype … the linguists were trained in california …

… i cannot imagine the difficulty of trying to break code today … we did it with a pencil … today computers make it impossible to crack in … we dealt with a very unsophisticated system form all the countrys communications we broke into … i was developing into a technician and intel pro … i felt very proud and privileged to be undergoing this training … i was still seventeen and had a top secret special intelligence clearance … now that really beat high school … we took several tests as we advanced along the course and with each one a student or two would be dropped from the course … but i was still there … the kid was doing it …

… finally the snow melted and we put away our overcoats for fatigue jackets … it was march and we were to graduate … then … just before graduation came that fateful day of receiving our assignments … i will never forget the assignments clerk announcing my name and saying sinop turkey … i would have to look at the map to see where that was … oh … i knew where turkey was but i never heard of sinop … i found it on the black sea coast on a peninsula that jutted out as the northern most town in turkey … on to the next great adventure i would arrive there three months shy of my eighteenth birthday … turkey …

… i noticed you go into the plural once in awhile … but you mention no names …

… i do not want to clutter up the tale …

… how did you feel about …

… what … how did i feel … come on you can ask a better question than that …

… yeah … i guess so … sounds kind of shrinkie does it not …

… yes … really … however you have a point … i did not spend a lot of time in my head … that would come later … much later … how did i feel about turkey …

… yes …

… it was a surprise to me … i never thought i would end up in such a faraway place … i was fired up about it …

... turkey ...

... it was not long from the time of graduation until five of us started our trek to sinop ... but first we had to go back to the repo depot at fort dix new jersey ... staying there a few days gave me the chance to visit my basic training company ... the old world war two barracks looked forlorn to me ... it was but seven months from the time i left there until returning ... by now i had settled into the army ... my training was complete ... now i had a job to do ... the replacement detachment was a bustling convergence of troops going all over the world ... one guy was going to thule greenland ... he was army security agency and therefore i did not ask what he was going to greenland for ... being army security agency i knew better than to ask ... also the insignia on our left shoulder got the attention of the staff ... oh ... these guys ... except for formations to go to meals we were left alone ... we had our days to ourselves and walked all over the place ... to the px ... to watch training going on with the new recruits in basic ... the sergeants did not treat us as recruits ... we were recognized as trained soldiers ... our demeanor was confident ...

... that is the best word i could use to describe myself ... confident ... we were there about five days until we got our orders to fly out from idlewild airport ... it had not been renamed j f k ...

... my second flight ... halfway around the world ... i was given tickets for everything ... the bus rides and the flight ... we were even given travel money to defray cab expenses and meals ... i should point out that i was making about a hundred dollars a month but it was all spending money ... lodging and food were taken care of ... i was a private first class with one stripe on my sleeve ... i thought it was as good a being a full colonel … it took me awhile to get in the mindset that a promotion was not worth anything … but that was way in the future …

… off to the big airport we go … we got there early and checked our bags so we did not have to fool with them … we went for a beer in the lounge … the drinking age in new york was eighteen at the time … no one carded me since i was in uniform … someone was supporting the troops and the beer was free …

… the airline we traveled on no longer exists … it was pan am … after the little plane i took to boston this one seemed huge … and it was only about half full … there were about ten or so in uniform … several were air force on the way to turkey also … we had a lot to talk about … but none of the conversations divulged what we did or what our training was … looking back it seems strange that the army would expect a seventeen year old to keep his mouth shut … but security was so engrained in us … i thought it was fun to be a spy … essentially that is what we were …

… off we went to our first stop in europe … paris … now i could say i was in paris but it was at the airport and only for two hours … i was struck by the people … there were travelers from all over the world … i just sat and watched the people coming and going … this was so different from america … it was not a little different … it was a great difference … the french were incredibly attractive people … the women were gorgeous … i probably sat there with my mouth open … then i dawned on me … i looked more european than not … i was german on one side and italian on the other … my italian side had only one generation separating me from rome and milan … plus i had a very european name … in the grandeur of this moment i felt i was one of them … i had a pastry and a cup of coffee … i did so because that is what the locals in front of me were having … i can give that experience as the time i got addicted to coffee … hey i was one of them … then off to our next stop … my grandmothers birthplace … rome … when we got back on the plane it was full … a couple of hours and i would be among the italians … my cousins … that airport was also fun to just sit and watch … again gorgeous people and so well dressed … i came to the conclusion that americans dressed like rag bags compared to europeans and this was in the early sixties … another two hours … another coffee and cake and on the way to athens …

… things were a little different there … a marked difference … if i had to label it … well … i would say there was a darkness to the atmosphere … the airport had a waft of cigarette smoke to it … i smoked too and joined them in the lounge … again with the coffee … there was something about the coffee … enough with the coffee already …

… the airport was older and appeared old world … that was the way i would describe it … old world … rustic … then off to turkey … on to ankara … and then to sinop … my home for a year … merhaba means welcome in turkish … i had knowledge of where the country was on the map but i had no idea what was waiting for me … i could not wait …

… this was all a part of my illness … my mania served me well … how many seventeen year olds would end up in turkey as a code breaker … i was glad my mother signed for me … i could have been sitting in high school bored by trigonometry .

… coming in low over the house tops i looked down upon old building and narrow streets … the city looked like something out of the movie the third man … yeah … it was rustic … but in my mind there was something sinister about it … it was a city of eastern european spies … russian agents … and secrets from the time of emporer constantine … i was flying into a james bond movie … my mind went into overdrive with the possibilities for adventure … you see … before i joined the army i saw doctor no and read from russia with love … i do not believe in the old adage of culture shock … what was to become shocked about … just look around and down at the cradle of the eastern roman empire … hey … romans were italian … this goombah was going to have a good time … we landed in the capitol … now what … i hoped someone would meet us there … merhaba abey … hello brother …

… my stay in ankara was three days … it was a whirlwind of in processing but we did have a little time to strike off on our own … i took a pamphlet from the hotel with me so i could get back by cab if i got lost … i did take a side trip to the tomb of the father of turkey … attaturk … mustafa kimel … i was impressed as to the modernization of an old city … large stone building built at the beginning of the seljuk turks taking over the city a century ago and the modern traffic signals and lighting … i went to a mall and was impressed at all the different goods from just about every european country especially france … thus was my introduction to metropolitan turkey … on to sinop …

… back out to the airport for a plane ride with turk hava yollari the turkish airlines … it was a prop job and i was glad to see clear weather … i would be able to site see from atop the countryside … i was going to samsun air base with two others … we made our trek together from devens to our new home … it was about a two hour flight and i saw the terrain change from flat farm land to rugged mountains … when we landed we saw nothing but hills and rock … no trees … taken by van to the air force mess hall we were told we would be on the way overland to sinop in a matter of hours …the trip would take us into the middle of the night on a six hour journey …

… we took off in an army truck and bounced over a dirt road along the side of the mountains … i was glad to see darkness fall as the truck slowed a bit and i could no longer look down the hundreds of feet drop-offs … out of sight out of … well … you get it … we pulled into what appeared to be a barnyard … it was a house with a dimly lit cellar … the turkish driver told us we were stopping for the restroom and a late meal … oh the meal … it was a bowl of sardines swimming in olive oil and a piece of bread … the bread must have been placed on a newspaper to cool as the bottom had news print on it … when in turkey do as the turks … the drink was a good red wine … after half an hour we were on our way for the last two hours of the journey … our bellies full we nodded off … no longer worried about falling to our death over the mountain passes … soldiers adapt … i could not see too much of the post as we pulled through the gate … a turkish soldier manned the gate and waved us through … we were taken to a quonset hut and told to off load … we were by this time bone tired and wanted to get into the rack … we picked out a bunk and the linen was already on the bed … come to find out a turkish housekeeper worked in each one of the barracks …

… no hurry for the in processing i guessed as we were allowed to sleep in … about ten a sergeant came in and told us that we had the day to ourselves and to take a look around and thus we did … we were also told that the quonset hut was temporary lodging … he pointed out the px and enlisted club and left us on our own … soon a friend of ours from devens showed up … he had gotten to sinop about a week earlier … he was glad to see us and explained about the place … there was a village down at the bottom of the hill but nothing to do except go to an outdoor café and drink tea … we had just gotten there and took a few minutes to put up our gear … we asked the sergeant if we could go downtown … he replied it was fine with him … we changed into civilian clothes and off we went … the dirt road down to the village was rocky and full of potholes … it seemed to me outside of the cities it was all dirt roads … out of the blue a cab swings up in front of us to take us to town … later we were to find out it was the only cab in sinop … a bus line did run through the town … but other than small villages dotting the coast we were on a rock jutting out into the black sea … we were out in the middle of nowhere …

… we paid the cab driver a few lira for the ride from the post to the theater in the village … in halting english he told there was a magic show and a movie in town … why not … we paid about a dollars worth of lira to enter the theater … the seats were stone benches formed in a semi circle the magic show was nothing to write home about but the movie … in turkish of course and not a word to be understood … anyway … the movie was a love story … but hey … it was entertainment … we walked out of the theater into a very dimly lit village … how to get to the road back to the post was our problem … we walked by a guard at what looked like an army office … he could tell we were a bit lost … he waved to us and said just keep going until you will get to the road at the end of the village … and in perfect english ... seems he lived in new york city as a kid ... go figure ... we got back to the hut and settled in for the night ...

... in the morning we walked to the headquarters building ... a small two story building with a central hallway and offices on each side ... we were checked in by personnel and finance ... then came the clearance papers ... the sergeant that gave us our clearence forms and entry badges to the operations building was a fidget ... he was smoking a cigarette and chewing on a toothpick at the same time ... his right leg kept bouncing up and down while he typed away ... we had to sign papers that vowed of silence ... in a sense it made us pledge not to talk about the activities in the operations building anyplace but in the operations building ... he was a pleasant enough sort but very distant ... he was one of those people who appear to have something to hide ... he appeared not to like his station in life ... maybe he did not like it on the post ... the post was known as the rock ... kind of a prison connotation ... after this in processing i only saw my other two travel partners in passing ... we were assigned to different shifts ...

... when i got to the operations building i was escorted inside by an mp ... different color badges meant you could only go into rooms marked with that color badge ... i had a blue badge giving me rights to all the rooms ... my idea at the time was that you could only see what you need to know ... my thoughts were i must need to know something in every room ... it made me feel privileged ... the first person i met was our section sergeant ... he gave me a tour of the building and then took me into my station ... it was a work station at the head of the morse code room ... i was to be an intercept controller ... it was then i found out about a fourth of our course at devens was based on the procedures at the sinop field station ... i was assigned to shift three ... the night shift ... the soldier i was replacing had about five weeks to train me ... i felt confident that it was enough time ... i was told to go back to the hut and try to get some sleep as i would be coming on duty at twenty three hundred hours ... eleven oclock ... and from now on i will not use military time in the few references i make to time ... at eleven that night i would start my work life ... i may have been in my teens but i had an adult job ... and i knew it ...

... looking back on it would you say that feeling european was a bit manic ...

... i did not look then as i do now of course ... i had black curly hair and this nose of mine ... well ... i fit right in in paris and rome ... at least it was fun to feel as though i fit in ... yeah that was it ... i was beginning to feel as though i fit in ...

... you did not feel that way at fort devens ...

... well ... i never have felt as though i fit in ... anywhere ... but this was something different ... i was in a foreign element and i wanted to fit in ... i thought it was cool to maybe fit in ... i am giving you the thought processes of me at that time ...

... so would you fit in now ...

... i do not know but i can tell you this ... i would not care ...

... you do not care if you fit in ...

... not anymore ...

... a boy no more ...

... the ops building was surrounded by antennas ... there were about two acres of antennas erected in a field to the east of the ops building ... all of them were pointed north ... it did not take a brain trust to figure out that we were listening in to networks in russia ... next to the ops building was a furnace ... we used it to burn our classified material ... it was one of our additional duties ...nothing classified left the compound ...

... i looked up sinop on the internet a few weeks ago and the background of the town was posted ... also ... just for hoots i typed in tuslog detachment four ... an lo and behold a web site popped up ... that was our official title ... turkish united states logistics ... tuslog ... again it was not all that hard to figure out that no logistics were being shipped anywhere ... there was no port just docks for fishing boats and no ship facilities ... just a good stretch of beach that we visited in the summer ... i got there in march and it was cold and raining all the time ... it was good to work indoors in the ops ... that was another thing that set us aside from most soldiering ... we work in fixed field stations ... we were indoor soldiers ... with the exception of conducting physical training and a trek to the rifle range once during my stay there ... it was all book work and transcribing text from messages copied in of room of morse code interceptors ...

... i had the intercept control of four radio networks ... about once a week they would change call signs and frequencies ... it was my duty to find them ... my job required me to read and decipher the externals of the messages ... i dealt with everything pertaining to but not involving the text of the message ... we had a separate section of cryptographers that dealt solely with the messages … my training was on the job … i was shown how to read the traffic which was standard world wide … the nets were also linked to voice and teletype … the linguists were in the next room and beyond that were the teletypes … but the room to the other side of the morse code room was the reason we were there … it was a dark room filled with electronics … that room was were the telemetry was captured …

… when the morse code traffic indicated that the nets were going operational … the intercept controler … me … would call the operations staff up … they were on call twenty four hours a day … as sometimes the nets would go operational several times a day … or in the middle of the night …

… here is the way it went … the morse nets would come up and send signals that indicated what the net was going to do … then the signal indicate the nets going operational … then the operational teletype nets would come up … when that happened they would go dual canal or sending and receiving at the same time … after which the linguists would search frequencies for the voice traffic …

… the telemetry room would come to life … and we would track their efforts on the other side of the black sea … it amazed me as to how easy it was to find them when they changed frequencies … and the other rooms were good at capturing them also …

… the first shift i came onto was the midnight shift or trick and it was my favorite shift … our trick chief was a specialist five … a very low rank to be in charge of all those folks and that mission … he was a very proficient morse interceptor and understood the functions of the other three rooms as well …

… i will bet you that when the detachment closed down in ninety two the trick chief was a captain … typical grade creep … but we had a very good guy for our boss … it made our life on the rock easier … not that it was hard to live there … i found it funny that our post doctor was a psychiatrist … a lot of the staff and operations soldiers were inclined to consider being stationed there a penalty … like they were locked up for doing something wrong … they expressed to me that they felt imprisoned … i never felt like that … i always thought of myself as an introverted person … but reflecting back on it … my ease in being stationed there was that i was comfortable with being withdrawn … i did a lot of things alone … i read a lot … i went to almost every movie that was shown in our small theater …no t v …

… we did however have a closed circuit radio station … and for awhile i was a d j on k b o k … that was the callsign of our station … bok is turkish for walk … as to walk out of the place …

… one thing good about the tour is that it was only a year … and we all had our next assignment to look forward to … i considered germany … let me digress … within limits we had our pick of assignments coming off of the rock … we were considered to be on a hardship and isolated tour … so i put in for panama … my buddy put in for taiwan … we knew we would get what we asked for …

… we had an enlisted mens club … and i use the word mens as there were no women on the post … it was nineteen sixty-four and the army had not expanded the role of women … the army would not until the mid seventies … we had a lot to do in the club … it had one armed bandits …and around payday each month some of the linguists would back casino games … this is where i learned i was not a gambler … i state today that i am not a good gambler … i like my hard earned money too much … but each payday i would play just enough to be up a little and then i would quit … i have always gambled like that … there is a stage where you will be up and that is a good time to quit … even if it is a couple of percentage points … quit … i did and came out ahead … i did lose a sure thing hand once for quite a bit … i did not evaluate an impossible hand that the other player may have had … i did not make that mistake again … it was the only time i can remember not being ahead when i quit … it was all luck as the house in casino games is always against you … that much i knew … the last night i was there i won a jackpot on the slots … i put a quarter in and pulled the handle … bam … a fifty dollar jackpot for twenty five cents … that was always the way i gambled …

… it i think … is unusual for a bipolar not to be pulled in by gambling … but i watched the people around me try to beat the odds

at the club and asked myself to come up with a good reason to do that
…

… sorry … got off track a bit …

… about halfway through the tour the troops were sent to trabson … an air force base … for a few days … just to get off the post and see some new terrain … i was never sent … in essence i was forgotten about … i looked at it a different way … i imagined the bosses thought i did not need to go off the post as i was doing all right … at least that is the way i justified being forgotten … this theme of being forgotten has plagued me all my life as you will read …

… it brought back an old memory of being forgotten on the roster of the football team in junior high … we were going to an away game and i was completely looked over for the team … i was very upset and brought it up to one of the other players … he took me to the coach and defended me as i was crying about being left off … i was angry at being forgotten … the coach laughed at me but told me i would be on the bus … i vowed to never beg like i did for being left out … that event made me pull inside of myself and i do not think i will ever get out of that … remembering that incident served me well and i did not bring being left out to the attention of my supervisors at sinop … i want to add something here … just jumping ahead a little … the football incident and the incident where i was forgotten about in sinop taught me a big lesson … it was a big hurt … hey … i was only eighteen and had no rank and knew too that i had no standing …

… *no standing* …

… i learned not to join things … no clubs … no associations … practically nothing got me as a member … i figured if i did not belong i would not be left out … sort of self protection from being snubbed … it has worked all my life … back to sinop …

… sinop was a very active mission … and during a three month period we were very short handed … so instead of four tricks and time off each week we worked three shifts and every day … it wore us down a little as we would have extra duties such a guard duty … we would walk around the one road we had in the compound and the turks patrolled the outside of the perimeter … it was one of those things that made no sense … we were guarding building that had staff in them twenty four hours a day … it looked to all of us like make work … that and our every day shifts would require us at time to be up and awake for as much as thirty six hours at a time … we would also have to fall out for alerts … we would be in our combat gear but were given no weapons … i considered all this as make work for officers that had nothing much to do … our whole operations staff had but three officers and a communications center officer … they rest just fiddled around … at least that was my opinion …

… as a young soldier my impression was that officers did not do much of anything … it is true however that the army is really run by sergeants … they keep the day to day functions of the army geared up and rolling along … with the exception of a few … we had a really great n c o staff …

… during my training at fort devens we were given leave over the holidays … this was my first christmas away from home … sinop had two turkish government functions … one was a prison and the other was an orphanage … over christmas we invited the kids up to have christmas dinner with us … only turkey was served … no ham,,, islam comes to the christmas tree … each child got a gift … they seemed pleased to be out of the orphanage for the day … maybe each of us lives on our own rock … i did not mind being away for the holidays … they passed without revelry in the club …

… when christmas rolled around i was getting short … i had less than ninety days and i received my orders for panama … my buddy got his for china … the thing that disappointed both of us was the lack of promotions … the staff told us that there were just no stripes to be had … they did not know who was getting promoted but it was not us … i never considered too much coming my way in the order of promotions … i really thought that i was the highest i could go … i was good at my duties and had confidence in myself … i had however no confidence that i would be recognized for it … but … much to my surprise i was given a letter of commendation for my file … i was so taken aback … me … a commendation … i must have read that letter a hundred times … i do not think anything i was awarded in the army mattered more than that one letter for my services … it was the best the staff could do … specialist four was not in my future at sinop …

… i did not have to suffer the long bouncy ride to samsun on the way out of country … i was flown out on a small army fixed wing aircraft … i was in samsun for about an hour until i caught a flight on turkish airlines flight to ankara … ah … ankara again … back to the same hotel to await the big iron bird back home …

… i had forty five days leave saved up and was going to take it all … i was not thinking much on that one … what was i going to do for forty five days … especially with as little pay as i had … oh well … from ankara to rome to paris to j f k … i had a roll and a coffee in rome and in paris … i was an old hand at international travel by now …

… it was the spring of sixty five and there was this place called viet nam ginning up … i knew nothing of it …

… that is funny … an old hand at international travel … let me ask you this … were you not wanting to tell people about what you did at sinop … i mean that is a fascinating story … just the little bit you told me … i guess you cannot tell me who it was you were listening in on …

… i probably could at this point in time … the soviet union having crumbled and all …

… so it was the soviets you were listening in on …

… cold war and all you know …

… and you became a night person …

… from my t v watching days i was pretty much a night person … along the way as i dealt with my illness i have met a lot of bipolars with an affinity for the night …

… just the way you presented this chapter you seemed to have matured a bit …

… oh … i think so … it was a very maturing experience …although i was still a kid i had been through a lot … being expected to perform …

… so that letter of commendation was a highlight of your career so far …

… you bet … it told me i was appreciated and respected … i learned that you do not have to have a lot of rank to be respected … that was one thing about this army security agency business … we did not have a lot of leaders that were trying to prove their power to you .,

… does that have anything to do with the fact that you had the run of the building and others did not …

… i did not think of it that way … i was not however given access to the code room where the cryptographers worked … that was the ultimate inner sanctum of the whole operation …

… the internals of the messages as you wrote about …

… yes … breaking out that code was all done by pencil and paper … it was all brainpower … p f c s breaking code … there is a funny story i just recalled .

… what …

… we … the intercept controllers on the shifts were working on breaking some callsigns to identify some stations of another facility that we copied … mostly during the evening and mids shift … we broke a few callsigns and identified the radio net … our work and direction finding pinpointed them … we turned the information over to the warrant officer in charge of code breaking … a few days later he called us in to his office and told us how well we had done … we were all proud of our work … then he told us not to do it again …

… why …

… it seems there were g s fourteens and high caliber people assigned the task of breaking the call signs and identifying the nets back at fort meade … they did not like being preempted by a bunch of army privates … it was my first run in with the bureaucracy …

… what did you do in response to that …

… i worked on our main mission and shied away from the secondary tasks … i did not want to have anything to do with the code breaking mission after that … before i put any identification in the reports i cleared them through our sergeant … the linguists and the teletype folks were a little gun shy also … i was beginning to understand why the national security agency was referred to as the puzzle palace …

… did it affect your work in the future …

... not really ... not as much as it did in sinop ... actually i tried to aggravate them when i could ... later on ... that is another trait of bipolar ...

... what is that ...

... finding a system against which to rebel ...

... something to look forward to and a system against which to rebel ... got any more gems like these ...

... more will be revealed ...

... re up ...

... at the little theater in sinop i saw the film ... the longest day ... i loved it and from then on i wanted to be a paratrooper ... i looked up to anyone with those jump wings on their chests ... once an idea gets in my mind ... well just like the army at seventeen thing ... i was focused ...

... i spent my time in pennsylvania and new jersey where my mother was now living ... i spent my leave bouncing around doing next to nothing ... in that environment i was back to smoking and staying up late to watch t v ... it was easy to fall back into the old habits ... i was a considerable distance from the kids around town in pennsylvania ... the guys had one thing hanging over their heads ... the draft was creeping up on them fast ... i came to realize i had two years in already ... time flew and i was much more secure and assured ... i had the confidence of an adult ... i was eighteen and on my way to my second overseas tour ...

... after those long six weeks i appeared at the orderly room door of the fort dix repo depot ... i was one of about five hundred in the company ... i was given the task of helping the operations sergeant ... it seemed there was one person going to panama ... me ... and five hundred going to germany on a troop ship ... i had to help process the germany bound soldiers ... and then i would be taken care of ... the sergeant had me over the barrel ... it was about a ten day stay ... i was fine with it ... i knew enough then to go along and get along ... he really appreciated my help and told me so ... he also told me that he picked me out to help him because i was army security agency and he always got good assistance from us ...

... i shook his hand and headed out on a plane to charleston south carolina ... i would be taking a military transport from the air base there to albrook air base in the canal zone ... i had a day lay over and spent the night in quarters that were like a hotel ... at fort dix i was in a barracks with seventy other guys ... here on the air force base i was i was given my own room and i was only a p f c ... the air force sure knows how to live ...

... awaiting the transport to load ... it was an airliner ... a contract flight ... a four engine prop job ... anyway ... this marine and i were sitting in the snack bar when an announcement came over the loudspeaker ... all draftees to parris island marine base go to the front of the terminal for bus transportation ... good grief ... we laughed ... getting drafted is one thing ... but into the marines ... katy bar the door ...

... i got to see cuba as we overflew it ... i found that surprising ... anyway it was about a seven hour flight to panama ... stepping off the plane ... no when i got to door of the plane ... wham ... i was hit with an oven like heat ... i was soaked in sweat by the time i walked to the terminal ... this was a huge contrast from turkey ... the place was a bustle with activity ... the army was separated from the air force and taken to a barracks on a post surrounded by palm trees ... we were told not to pick up any snakes ... great advice ... i really had no intention of getting near any snake ...

... i spent the night in the barracks and was taken over to fort clayton to the army security ageny barracks ... i was getting off the truck when out of the building comes a classmate of mine from fort devens days ... flip was his nickname ... his first question was ... what are you doing here ... i guess i did not leave a very good impression on him during training ... i told him i was coming in from sinop ... he was still a p f c ... i guessed the stripes did not come this way either ... i was later to find out that the stripes were reserved for the soldiers assigned to isolated posts ... what ... there is always a made up reason for everything ...

... it was not long before i was able to go down town ... panama city had all the charm of a mexican border town ... now i had never

been to a border town but i imagined this is what it would look like …
riding the bus into town there were some chinese speaking spanish …
go figure … i guessed it was the same as chinese speaking english …
the canal zone was one big sprawling base … fort after air base after
fort … the canal zone was in all respects a big city …

… it was a few days until i would be working in operations …
another windowless building adjacent to a huge antenna field …

… i may as well have been on mars instead of sinop … the place
was overrun with rank and i was quickly advised that i did not have
any … sergeants and staff sergeants were doing the work that a p
f c was doing in turkey … the big question was that if i was on an
isolated tour why was i still a p f c … i quickly felt like a second class
citizen i withdrew into myself … i was there about two weeks before
i was ready to leave …

… i asked about going airborne … becoming a paratrooper and
getting assigned to our special forces unit across the isthmus … that
got a good laugh … i was told i could only do that in the states … my
brain went to overdrive it …

… panama was also my first experience with other soldiers
from other disciplines … from the airborne unit at fort kobe to the
supply unit next door … it reinforced my belief that even though this
assignment appeared to suck … i was still a lot better off than the
rest of the army … the army security agency was in my mind a pretty
good deal …

… again i was assigned to a trick … we would work a week on
days then swings then mids … i was given the job of trying to identify
radio nets from all over central and south america … it was a no
brainer most of the time as they sent their messages in plain text …
what we were copying was unclassified radio traffic … i could have
sat in the p x and done that … there was no urgency to our mission …
i got the opinion that the folks assigned here were on a big vacation
… i felt useless really quickly … for some odd reason we copied ship
traffic in the canal … a great effort was made to identify them … i
asked why we just do not run down to the canal and read the name off

the ship and look at the flags to see who it is registered to … that met with sour looks …

… i had two gambling events … there was an upscale section of panama city and there was a casino … i was curious and decided to pay the place a visit … it was swanky to say the least … i went to the crap table and decided against that as the action moved to fast for a study of the odds … i went to the blackjack table plunked down a whole dollar and won … looked like easy picking to me … i realized the odds were in favor of the house but i thought i would stay with it awhile … in no time i was up forty dollars … now that may not sound like too much but it was a quarter of a month s pay … i got out at forty … i decided to save the forty for other gambling …

… not to long after that i got involved in a barracks poker game … it was a quarter fifty cent game and i watched all the players stay in with bad hands … they were trying to make a hand on the last two cards … if i did not have a developing hand in the first three cards of seven card stud i folded … they did not figure it out that i only stayed in if i had a good hand … i soon relieved them of about a hundred dollars … these were not very friendly guys and i had little to do with them in the course of my duties … one guy was completely wiped out for the rest of the month … i was going to give him his money back … i decided against that as it may have insulted him … after the game we went down town and i bought the first round … they loosened up to me a little but it was a clique i did not wish to hang out with … i did have a buddy nicknamed chepis … he was the only one that did not roll his eyes when i said i was going airborne …

… i did eventually get promoted to specialist four … i felt the promotion had no value … if it was worth anything it would not be given to me … i was falling into a deep depression but as luck would have it i was assigned to escort classified material … there were two of us and one had to be armed … there was a sergeant assigned to that duty and then he would just take one of us with him … i had no idea what was in the briefcase … it was probably ships identified by our operations … anyway he was assigned to personnel and we got to talking about him being airborne … the paratrooper thing again …

… i asked him if i could go back to the states to go through the school … he said no to that … but i could re-up you know reenlist to go to the special forces unit at fort bragg … but would i not have to finish my tour in panama … no he said … my tour in panama would be curtailed … i would have jumped out of the plane without a parachute to get that assignment …

… i reenlisted and in two months was on the way to fort bragg north carolina … a green beret was in my future …

… i took a lot of flack for going to jump school … a lot of my fellow soldiers in panama told me i would never make it … i had doubts myself … i was impressed by the fact that they wished me ill … they did not want me to make it … i guess to prove themselves right …

… this sort of thinking on the parts of others was to follow me through all of my volunteering for training … oh you cannot do that … it brought up old stuff … at home before i came in the army i would announce i was going out for a sport or going to be in some school activity … i would be told that i could not do that … when it came to sports they were right … the airborne training brought up that old feeling …

… i was glad to be wheels up in panama … on the way to fort bragg … with two overseas tours under my belt i hoped i would be received as a trained and experienced soldier …

… *were you* …

… no …

… no longer a straight leg …

… going into grannis field was the only time in all my world travels that my bags were lost … when i inquired about what to do … the guy at the baggage counter told me maybe they will be in tomorrow … to check back … maybe …

. a soldier from my unit was there picking up an officer and offered me a ride to my unit … i got into the place with nothing but the clothes on my back … i had to try to get a ride back to the airport the next day … i got up early … it was a sunday … i called to see if my bags were in and they were … they had been there all the time … i asked a guy in the barracks if he would take me down … i offered him a tank of gas … when we arrived at the airport my bags were sitting out on the curb … just sitting out there for anyone to run off with … i got lucky …

… being in an airborne unit as a non jumper was to be a second class citizen … it would be a month before i would be going to jump school …

… i was enthused to begin the mission … there was none … no really … a detachment of about twenty five soldiers and no reason for being … all we did was look busy … we were given very little to do and there was no training … there were some soldiers there that were sergeants that never had been on an assignment with a mission … i was very disappointed … in fact i was very bored … my past experience counted for nothing … all the unit did was walk around with a beret on … then i went to jump school …

… this was my first introduction to tactical training … the school is divided into three one week increments … ground week was the basic techniques of landing and hard physical conditioning … i passed through that training … and moved on to tower week … we would jump from a thirty four feet tower to simulate jumping from a plane … after jumping we would slide down on a cable to a mound about thirty yards from the tower … unhook and come back and make another jump … friday of that week we were to fall from the two hundred fifty feet tower …a parachute was rigged up to a round metal ring and once hooked up and in our harness … up we would go … hanging there a couple of hundred feet in the air was a frightening sensation … i will not tell you that i was not scared of all this … but i plugged along with the program …

… then came jump week … monday was to be our first jump but the weather was too bad … as well as tuesday … we were told we would make two jumps on wednesday and two in thursday … our final jump would be on friday rigged with combat equipment …

i will never forget that first jump … we went into the plane … an old c one nineteen of korean war vintage … by rank order with an officer as a stick leader … the line of jumpers was referred to as a stick … i was the senior enlisted man in the stick so i got to enter first which made me the last out of the airplane … we would make two passes over the drop zone … i got to watch each jumper in front of me exit the door … the noise of the engines and rush of the slipstream created a loud howling … i could barely hear the sergeant … the jumpmaster … i considered just sitting down and saying the heck with it … but i did not and that was my moment of truth … that was one of those times in ones life when a decision has a marked effect on the rest of your years … soon there was a gaping hole in front of me … it was the open door … out i went … the chute opened just fine and … well … to tell you the truth … it was like a big carnival ride … a big carnival ride …

… i distinctly remember the second jump as well … several of my classmates quit the course before the second jump … the third and forth jumps have not stuck in my mind … the fifth however does … as it was a combat equipment mass tactical jump … we were rigged with a weapon and combat pack … the pack was strapped below the reserve which fit waist high … the mass tactical part meant that the sky would be filled with jumpers … when i landed on that fifth jump i was qualified to get my wings … i was a paratrooper …

… when i got back to the unit i was taken into the fold of the airborne soldier … i was no longer referred to as a leg or a straight leg … the term comes from none airborne soldiers wearing shoes instead of jump boots … thus there trousers are straight … or straight legged … i was no longer a leg …

… i waited until i had a couple more jumps under my belt before i sent a post card to the trick back in panama … i had made it through the school … i doubted myself and made it … i wanted them to know if for no other reason than my own self satisfaction … and to prove them wrong of course …

… still though … nothing to do … to tell you how bad it was i volunteered to paint the stripes on the tennis court …

… i did get to go to mountaineering training … climbing off of rocks and rappelling … i did not take to it right away … i did not trust the equipment … but through the training i was able to get it together and started to climb and rappel along with the others … it turned out to be a macho thing … i was getting more macho … you might call it swaggering … but down inside i knew i was in a position of nothing … it seemed to me these guys were satisfied to do nothing except fatigue details … i was wearing a green beret … the song of the same name was number one in the nation …

… i knew the berets in viet nam … commonly called the forces … i knew they had a great rep … but it was not so … at least not for my current assignment …

… then my focus turned to getting out of the place … i had a situation with my mother … she wanted to come down and live there … she told me that since she took care of me for seventeen years i could now take care of her … my aunt got all over her for that and forbade her to come down … what my aunt wants my aunt gets … but from then on i was bound to get overseas and there was one place that i could get to very fast … from the time i put in paperwork until i was at the repo depot fort dix new jersey was less than two months …

i was on my way to viet nam … talk about something to look forward to …

… i spent four days at fort dix until i was manifested to a flight that would go from the adjacent air base … i have to think a little … it was mcguire air force base … it was a charter flight and it would go from jersey to alaska … then into tokyo … to the philippines and on to tan son nhut air base outside of saigon … we were not let off the plane in japan but all the other stops we could stretch our legs … a world traveler again … it took nineteen hours of travel time … with the down times to refuel the trip took twenty seven hours … i was too excited to get jet lag …

… when we landed we were taken into a pavilion and each of our names were called off with our assignments … i knew i was going to the third radio research group … a thinly veiled name for the army security group … the group was on the air base … we were assigned to buses and loaded up within a few hours …

… i was impressed that the buses had screens on the windows and we had a military police escort with jeep mounted m sixty machine guns … i asked why the screens and was told it prevented the viet cong from throwing grenades into the bus … hello … well now jon you are in viet nam … the buses took us to a tent city that was a repo depot … we were divided by rank … i was told to get into the group of non commissioned officers … sergeants … i had arrived to a status of career soldier as i had been promoted at fort bragg … do nothing get promoted … that was about what it amounted to … and i had a feeling there was a lot more in my future than to paint rocks ala fort bragg style … we were told that we would spend the night in the depot and would be assigned the next day … it was all right with me … i needed a little sleep and some food … this was the first time that i was not in a hurry to have a look around … grenades through the bus windows had gotten my attention … also we were warned as to what to do should a mortar attack take place … essentially it was to dive on the ground and hope a direct hit does not come your way … we were told of past attacks … this was my in country introduction … the vietnamese that worked in the compound all wore tops and pants that resembled pajamas … they were all incredibly thin and short … they looked poor …

… the mess hall was staffed by the vietnamese … the whole place was staffed by the vietnamese … as it turned out the military was the biggest employer in vietnam …

… in our briefing we were told there were one hundred twenty five thousand united states troops in viet nam … that number would swell to gargantuan proportions in the year i was there … it was march of sixth six … i was as they say … in country …

… did you feel prepared for the experience …

… not really … i had a little training while at fort bragg but nothing to do with war or fighting as an individual soldier … thinking back on it i found all that type of training not to be very useful in the real world of being in a combat zone … it seemed to me that all training was for infantry missions in europe … the army constantly fought the last war …

… what was the big difference in viet nam …

… at this stage … my recent arrival … i really had no understanding of the type of enemy we were up against … so far my experience was to hit the ground if we got mortared and someone may throw grenades at me … i understood basic soldiering from my initial training and the only thing i knew about the mission in viet nam was from two sergeants in sinop … they were assigned to a field station and reported to the national security agency … so i thought it would be much like sinop … being a paratrooper was a benefit to me … i got real lucky … actually i made my own luck …

… you seem to have a knack for doing that …

… i was useless for a year between the panama tour and fort bragg …

… useless … you thought of yourself as useless …

… yeah … if i had nothing to do … or what i was doing did not matter … well i did not matter … i was depressed for a year … landing in viet nam got me out of that funk … i did not know i was in it until i got out of it …

… did you think of it like that …

... i did not know if i was cut out for tactical units ... there were two strata of the army security agency ... tactical units ... and field stations ... my last assignment was the four oh third army security agency detachment with the special forces... i had no idea where i would be assigned ...

... but being a paratrooper was an advantage ...

... you will see ...

... more will be revealed ...

... finding the enemy ...

... the call came over the repo depot loudspeaker ... all those to the third radio research to the front gate in fifteen minutes ... it took me about three to get there ... i had the idea if i was not there i would not be mortared ... i know it sounds silly but i was tired and was sort of dull ... i guess i did have jet lag ... only three of us showed up ... we loaded on a truck and were driven about four city blocks into a compound with the third r r u painted on a design over the gate ... we unloaded our duffle bags and were told to go into the orderly room ... by this time i had removed my beret ... i did not want to wear it as there were no army security agency special forces troops in country ... we were met by the first sergeant and handed a stack of forms to fill out ... he told us do not put third r r u in the assignment block as we were all going up country ... whatever that meant ...

... up country did not mean north ... it meant we were not staying at the field station ... we were all going to tactical units ... from the orderly room we were directed to personnel ... it was there we were given our assignments ... one to the twenty fifth infantry division ... one to the first infantry division and me to the one seventy third airborne brigade as i was jump qualified ... little did i know it was a luck out assignment ...

... i filled out a form for finance and that was it ... i was ready to go up country ... not long after that i ran into my old commander from fort bragg and he was wearing a one seventy third patch ... he told me to grab my gear and come along ... first we went to the tan son nhut p x and then on our way to bien hoa ... pronounced ben wah ... we drove through a suburb of saigon called gia dinh ... sections of the town were colonial houses but as we got to the outskirts of the town the houses were shacks made of tin from shipping containers … open cooking stoves were in front of most of the houses … this was the slums … after we passed through gia dinh we crossed a bridge about a quarter mile in length and after that it was flat land and rice paddies … about twenty minutes after the bridge and headed northbound there was a large installation to the west … it went on for miles … it was known as long binh and it would become one of the largest installations in viet nam … it was set up to receive thousands of troops later on in the year … the post was dotted with tents and huts made of screen wood and tin on the roofs … they were referred to as s e a huts for southeast asia … we turned east past more tin shacks and then the road became tree lined … the trees were left over from the french … then the town of bien hoa came into view … it was a town of more colonial homes and shops and restaurants … there were bars and tailor shops … bicycle shops and kiosks for food and drinks … the roads were paved … that alone made the town upscale as i would learn later … we turned right onto a winding road past a vietnamese army guard post … the two soldiers waved us on …then we approached another gate with the one seventy third insignia on a sign above the gate … the m p waved us through and then to the right about two city blocks and i was home … i jumped off the truck and a lieutenant told me to pick any tent … there was a row of tents for barracks and two large tents put together to make up the operations and communications center … a shower stall and toilet were set off from the ops tent … there were two buildings … s e a huts … one was for the club house and the other was the supply room … i was told to go to the supply room and get a weapon … the first thing i was issued at the four oh fourth was an m sixteen … that was my unit designation … the four oh fourth radio research detachment airborne … yeah … i was in an airborne unit … after getting my rifle i was taken to the brigade supply depot and was issued field gear for field operations … that took up the afternoon and pretty well filled up my day … i was introduced around and then taken to the operations tent … the a o … area of operations was on a maps posted on a big map board … i was told the brigade had the largest area of operations in the country as we always worked with other units … mostly the divisions … but as the war went on we would be operating alone … the brigade was not at full complement … we had two infantry battalions and for a third battalion we had a royal australian regiment … the aussies were right up the dirt road from us … it was getting dark and we were bedding down for the night … i kept hearing these explosions off in a distance … i was curious as to what it was …

… i thought it was bombing but upon inquiring was told the noise was the brigades artillery fire … little did i know that i would be very familiar with the artillery as my tour went on … the next morning my head was clear from the jet lag and was told i had to go back down to the third r r u for a few more processing details … i was able to take in more of the countryside as we drove back in to tan son nhut … it was not a problem getting me back down for the paperwork … seems the troops wanted to go to the air base and use the p x … there was one stretch of road that we seemed to speed along a little faster … i asked why and was told that it was an area where snipers operated … oh great … mortars and now snipers … i was quickly getting the idea that this was unlike any other army security agency experience …

… after completing my processing we went back that evening … as we passed through gia dinh again i noticed that all the little shacks had light … my thought was … how can an electric company keep all that straight … dah … they just siphoned the power off the lines leading into the city … the vietnamese were ingenious as i would find out later … their way of life was not a destitute as i thought it would be … they were not poor … it was that their standard of living was much different than ours …

… anyway … when we got back i was to learn that an operation was being ginned up … i was told to go to the operations tent with another code breaker and get briefed on the operation … i was also told i would not be going out right away as i was expected to be up on the mission of the four oh fourth … i was to learn that this was a real low level mission … by that i mean it was not important to report things to group all the time … many of the radio nets we worked with were not identifiable … many radio nets were small tactical units of viet cong … perhaps only three to five viet cong in what was known as a cell … our main mission was to locate the radios by direction finding … most of the direction finding was accomplished by aircraft over the areas of operation … finding them was the hallmark task … identifying the major units was also a mission but that was very difficult given the low level of communications sophistication … they were operating with morse code on low power radios … perhaps battery operated or with a little hand crank generator …

… one thing that was to be foremost in our operations was that these guys were all around us … among us and very hard to find … the viet cong meaning vietnamese communists were hard to pin down … we labeled the units with squad and platoon and company and battalion and regimental size … but it was just a designation … we had no idea of the real size of the units … i got to believe their battalions were no more than a hundred or so … ours were six hundred … and that was about the ratio needed to hunt them down … six to one … if we could even do it with that …

… what i am disclosing to you was of minimal classification … and eventually as the information was briefed to the brigade commanders and staff it became unclassified … we were after the regiments designated the two seventy second two seventy third and the two seventy six … these guys carried rusty rifles from the last war with the french … eventually they were supplied from the north and were issued a k forty sevens and rockets on top of the mortars they already had … with all of our technology we were not able to pin them down … my first impression of these guys was that to be that good they had to be dedicated … i knew they were communists and were trying to take over the country … my mind set at the time was how were they going to do that with what they had … we had tanks and helicopters and artillery and an endless supply … we would have these guys whipped in a year … hah …

… in the four oh fourth i was an exception … to my surprise most of the soldiers were not jump qualified … not to me but to the brigade they were in that second class category … plus we were not doing any jumping as there was a lack of available aircraft … but we still got our jump pay … back to the mission …

… we were issued crypto pads … one time use tablets for the communications of our direction finding units … we had the planes but the four oh fourth also had equipment know as p r d ones … portable direction finder type one … they were low range but were very useful for finding those low level units … if they were communicating in our t a o r … tactical area of operations … we would find them … but we learned this … when they communicated they also moved … so we would have to get on top of them quickly …

… on the first operation i made sure the unit in the field got all the direction finding pertaining to us … i keep a date time line of the map board … concentrations of communications sites may indicate a larger unit … i gave the information to the brigade intelligence staff and if there were no troops in the vicinity the artillery was called in on the location with a follow up from the cavalry … the cavalry was a helicopter unit … the cavalry was responsible for security reconnaissance and economy of force … they were the forward eyes and ears of the brigade … together with the long range recon unit assigned to them … they were the in the air and on the ground in contact with the viet cong … and they got fifty percent of their contact information from the four oh fourth … i was in it now … after over a year of nothing this was a real mission … the best i ever had …

… the next operation i went on and we got to the operation site by convoy … we convoyed by day to avoid ambushes … i am not saying that we could not move at night but the commanders thought it prudent to go over the road in daylight … all the while we moved the cavalry patrolled in the air above us and ahead of us …

… we got to the operations site and set up our tent … we always set up a tent to keep the equipment dry … we put the p r d one teams out at two different sites so their direction finding would give us what was known as a cut … we would plot the location and the direction of the radio signal they found and the lines would cross … the two lines made a cut … three lines made a fix … a fix was more accurate … the aircraft made a fix when possible …

… each day as part of my duties i went to the commanders briefing … i was one of the few enlisted men to go to the briefing … but at times i was the senior soldier at the field ops … i was nineteen years old and deep into the mission of my third overseas tour … sinop turkey was a great mission but viet nam had a worthy purpose and i felt a part of a team … the brigade was the first time in my life i felt a part of something bigger than myself …

… do not tell me you were wrapped up in yourself more than what was around you …

… as i look upon it now … my thought processes back then … yeah … i was always involved with myself … but viet nam was a greater purpose … i think … now of course as i look back on it … for my youth my tour with the brigade was probably the healthiest period of my life …

… what made you get out of yourself …

… selfishness …

… how so …

… when you are under the gun so to say … things get put into perspective … there was a survival element to the way of life over there …

… i can understand that …

… the cavalry helicopters were parked across from us and one rainy night viet cong came through the wire and put satchel charges under two copters … they blew up and sent shards of metal into our area … the shards came through the tents and hit three of our troopers … one … our ops sergeant was hit in the abdomen and had intestines hanging out … another was hit in the back and another in the arm … our unit got three purple hearts that night … i was lucky … i was lying down and just rolled over onto the floor when the explosions went off and the stuff flew over my head …

… i got the idea that paratroopers ought to jump … i had thirteen jumps and wanted to get more … especially in viet nam … i thought it would be cool to have a set of vietnamese army jump wings … so one day just on a lark i called the viet nam airborne division and asked if we … a couple of us in the four oh four … well i asked if we could jump along with their troopers … the operations sergeant said we could come on down the next morning and jump a c forty seven … that was an old world war two aircraft … it would be vietnamese parachutes vietnamese aircraft and vietnamese pilots … off we went in the dark of night to tan son nhut air base to load up and jump … by this time i was all about patches on my uniform … i thought the more patches one had the better your fatigues looked … anyway … off we went and that morning jumped a dakota for our wings … to this day i have the certificate on my wall presenting me my vietnamese wings … it was four days before i turned twenty … i was to make two more jumps in country with the brigade … but i hold the memory of that jump from a c forty seven in my head to this day … it is as vivid as my first jump …

… you did that for a patch on your uniform …

… yeah … it looked great on my fatigue shirt …

… you did not talk about the commanders … i take it they were a radical difference from the … … not radically different … sorry to interrupt … let me tell you about the brigade commander that was there when i got to the four oh fourth … he was a very seasoned officer … a brigadier general … a one star … i learned his history … he was in the second world war with the hundred first airborne division … two combat jumps and the stand at bastogne … he commanded a company of paratroopers … he also served in the korean war … i thought all in the world of him …he did not strut and was not at all impressed with himself … he was impressed with the mission … and he got the word out to the troops … everyone on the mission … on the operation … was briefed as to the reason for the operation … we felt informed and ready to meet the challenge on all the missions …he was promoted to major general and left the brigade … i do not think he was comfortable with the war … he was not reluctant but there was something about him that spoke to us about the war … he was an old asia hand and had served as an advisor to the nationalist chinese … he retired soon after he got back to the states … i think he was retired for political reasons …

… not one hundred percent behind the war …

… he may not have been but our detachment was … it was early in the war and we felt a true sense of purpose … we had a seasoned captain as our commander …he was a korean war vet … he was good for us as he got things done and supported the troops … he gave me the impression he was there to get the job done and not pump up his career … during his command he got us s e a huts instead of the tents … we had an operations building with stations set up to copy the viet cong nets … we were getting information that was above the tactical level and we were reporting to the puzzle palace … at our battalion operations we had a very good reputation … about half way through the tour we got a battalion as our next in command … so we reported from detachment to battalion to group … the reason for the expansion in command was the expansion of troops in country …

… how much …

… we were on several operations that supported the security of troops being brought into the country … an armor regiment … several infantry brigades … and two divisions were brought in … with that expanded the radio research units … and thus the battalion … let me tell you it was cool to go over to battalion with jump wings … vietnamese jump wings and the brigade airborne patch on … all the combat units … those with the brigades and divisions were well thought of by the battalion … my impression was that the battalion had a good staff … i knew the operations sergeant from sinop … after awhile i got the impression that the army security agency was a tight club especially for the career soldiers … then i got an idea …

… uh oh …

… yeah i got focused again …

… how so …

… i had a few helicopter flights and loved it … flying low level and looking at the terrain … they were so agile … i also looked up to the young warrant officer pilots and thought that they were not much older than me … i talked to the executive officer and asked him if he would help me apply for warrant officer flight school … he had one better … why not apply for officer candidate school and then to flight school … go to flight school as an officer … officer candidate school was just shy of six months and then on to the nine month aviators course … i thought it over for about ten minutes and decided to apply … it was a mountain of paperwork … but i plunged into it and had an application ready to go in a week …

… *wait a minute … you were not even a high school graduate …*

… i know but that was not a requirement … i had passed the officer candidate test and thus qualified to go … i asked that i be able to finish my tour and the command over at battalion told me that would be the case anyway … in about four months i had orders to report to fort benning georgia to o c s … it was the infantry school … i had been there for jump school and knew the system … fort benning is real tight as far as the commands go … it was all spit and polish … actually i thought it was a little overkill as to the way the officers and sergeants acted … since i knew what i was getting into i was not intimidated … plus i knew i would be one of the most experienced in the company … i was right as to that … my year was up and i took the big iron bird home … by far it was my best experience in my four years of service … i now had a combat patch for my uniform … the airborne brigade was well respected in the states as well … i also had four decorations on my chest … i really liked collecting badges patches and now medals …

… *sounds like you did a year in a manic state …*

… mania served me well … i seemed to excel in mania … of course i did not know it was mania at the time …

… *did you go back home for another forty five days as you did from turkey …*

… nope … stayed for about two weeks … i was treated a little differently …

… *how so …*

… i had been through an experience unlike anyone in the family had been through … at this point i will say i had matured beyond my years … i was not yet twenty one … there is something about the stress of what i went through … the responsibility i had and the credit i was given for accomplishing the mission … that was it … i had accomplished the mission … and was on my way to becoming an officer …

… did you relate a lot of your experiences to the family …

… no … i talked about the people but i did not relate the time we got hit with the helicopters exploding … i did not relate the use of airstrikes and artillery on the viet cong … i kept it light … just hung around the house … my grandparents place …

… air strikes and artillery …

… yes … almost daily the targets i gave to the intelligence staff of the brigade ended up at least being hit by artillery … because of that i was a accurate as possible with the data … when you fire artillery you have to know where it is going …

… did you talk about your jumps …

… yes … but not the cancelled mission …

… cancelled mission …

…. yeah i forgot about that …

… mind telling me about it …

… let me see where to begin … i was on r and r in taiwan … and into about three of the six days … i went up to the army security station on the island to meet a guy i had served with in turkey … and while i was there a message was sent in to find me and send me back to the brigade … no reason why … just go back to the four oh four … i packed up and was on the way back in hours … someone got an extra day of r and r as they bumped him for me …

… i landed at tan son nhut … and knew immediately why i was called back … on one side of the taxiway the c one thirties were being rigged for jumping and on the other side stood a dozen or so vietnamese air force c forty sevens … what was up was a jump … now this is where the story gets good …

… keep going …

… our sister unit at the brigade was the military intelligence detachment … it seems one of the troopers was down town in a tailor shop and saw jump wings with a star embroidered on the canopy … he asked why that was and the tailor told him it was for the combat jump at bunard … an old french base … the thing was the jump was yet to go off ... the jump and the location had been compromised ... the trooper took some of the wings back to the brigade intelligence staff ... the mission was not cancelled but the brigade commander sent the cavalry copters to investigate ... it seems the drop zone was booby trapped ... we would have jumped on land mines ... the mission was cancelled ...

... how did the tailor find out about it ...

... we briefed the vietnamese staff of their airborne division ... they were in on the jump also ...

... so you think the word leaked out from them ...

... no doubt about it ...

... there were viet cong in the division ...

... well ... yeah ... there were viet cong in all the vietnamese units ... anyway ... i got beat out of a combat jump ...

... another badge ...

... yeah ... and when the next operation for a combat jump went off an officer from the field force staff took my spot ... that jump was just a little turning point in the war ...

... how so ...

... the mission was ... well ... compared to the combat jumps in the second world war this jump was a ... well it was concocted ...

... concocted ...

... yeah ... there was nothing there ... to me it was grandstanding ... plus i wanted to be on it ... but looking back on it ... it was a sham ...

... that is pretty strong talk ... this is the most heated i have seen you or read so far ...

... really ... i had mixed emotions ... it would have been a star on my wings to make the jump ... but was it really a combat jump ... there was no enemy there ... in fact there was nothing there ... ah ... the quest for badges and patches ... by the way that is an airborne trait ...

... what was an airborne trait ...

… to have a uniform so decked out with stuff you look like latin american general … i got over the whole combat jump thing and went on to fort benning …

... an officer yea really ...

... going from viet nam to officer candidate school at fort benning was going from squalor to pristine ... i knew what i was in for ... it would be a lot of yelling and intimidation and hoopla that had nothing to do with real leadership ... i reported in to the sixty first candidate company sixth battalion ... there were a couple of thousand officer candidates at benning ...

... i was more relaxed than most ... the first couple of days were processing and drawing gear ... everything was cut and dry ... it was a do this do that couple of days ... then we were assigned our permanent barracks space of a footlocker a desk a wall locker and a bunk ... the next morning is when it hit the fan ...

... at about four in the morning our platoon lieutenant came strutting in and yelling at us ... we jumped up and he had us run around all over the place for no reason at all ... allow me to digress ... this guy ... this lieutenant had about eight months in the army ... he had gone through basic training and officer s candidate school ... that was it ... he spent his whole time in training ... he was a glib brooklyn tough guy ... or at least he wanted us to think that ... i found him to be obnoxious ... but then i knew that was all he knew with just eight months in ... his whole time in the army was getting yelled at ... we had six lieutenants that were our platoon tactical officers ... one with a year in viet nam ... the rest were overnight lieutenants and all but one were screamers and yellers ... it was part of the game ...

... i knew it would be a long six months ... this was to be a mixed period for me ...

... *mixed period* ...

… yeah … manic and depressed …

… how did you cope with that …

… my mania allowed me to look forward to the day of graduation … my depression was from keeping myself in the present …

… i did not mean to interrupt …

… oh no you are not interrupting at all … i want you to ask these things … i get caught up in the tale and forget to relate to my illness …

… it seems to me your illness served you well … i mean you went from a private to an officer candidate very fast …

… the war was going on … the combat arms schools had to pump out as many officers as they could … we not only had viet nam we had europe and korea to staff … that is a key point about the training …

… how so …

… i wrote about it before … how the army was always fighting the last war … except we were fighting the last war we won … i do not remember korea being mentioned one time in our benning training … it is true … korea is the forgotten war …

… back to the training … the first four weeks were a lot of physical conditioning training and classes on the basics of the structure of the army … it was sort of like basic training two oh two … that was okay with me … it was good to review … there were six viet nam vets out of the original two hundred twenty eight … most of those who no longer wanted in the course quit in the first seven weeks …

… at the end of the seventh week a company formation was held to see who wanted to leave the course no questions asked … about a dozen stepped out of the formation … it was after that … after the sleepless seventh week that we started into the tactical training … all of the training up until the twentieth week was based on combat operations on the central european plain in the second world war … the course had n a t o on the brain … viet nam was talked about very little … many of the instructors had not had a tour in viet nam … especially the lieutenants …

… we would truck out to field sites for armor and artillery operations and we were all over the place for infantry tactics … we had very little instruction on the use of aviation … the infantry school treated the aviation units a second class citizens … then i got focused on my next step …

… applying for flight school after graduation … it was a cut and dried process as a lot of pilots were needed in viet nam … i had not doubt that if i went to flight school i was going right back to viet nam … but i applied anyway … and was accepted about a week before graduation … the thing was i could not go right after officer candidate school as i would have to wait for a class date …

… as i look back on officer candidate school i think of the talk i had with my executive officer in viet nam … i would be able to go to flight school as an officer … but first i would have to go through the drudgery of the infantry school … essentially i had made up my mind not to be an infantry officer but a pilot …

… you know what we have not talked about …

… what …

… you mentioned that when you went to jump school you were told you would never make it …

… i see where you are going … i took a lot of flack for applying to o c s … i heard a lot of the bit that i would not make it … but you know i never developed the i will show you attitude … i was in my own world … in my own movie …

… movie …

… i guess i never got into this with you … i treated everything i did as though i was in a movie role … i even made up theme music in my head … all the infantry field problems … well … i just played music in my head … i went through my tour with the brigade like that … on the operations i had theme music … on the jumps i had theme music …

… there is one way to look at it … you got a lot out of watching those late movies when you were a kid …

… true … i always had theme music going in my head … even when i wrote the draft of this book i had music on … i write best with theme music from the x files …

… the x files …

… but back then i had theme music from old war movies … the movies were a far cry from the real thing … but the music was good …

… the toughest thing about o c s for me was the lack of imagination … there were set ways to conduct operations and i could not divert from the manual … i always thought that if we had the manual to read so could the other side … if the other side read the book than they knew what we were going to do … it was true for the entire branch … the infantry was the infantry … not a bunch of pilots …

… week after week of the spit shine and the training soon brought the last three weeks of training when we were senior candidates … the other candidates had to salute us … i had been an enlisted man for so long i felt odd being saluted … and i have to tell you this … my grandparents my aunt and my mother came down for my graduation … i was pleased with that … perhaps i was not doing so bad after all …

… i graduated in december of sixty seven … the war was foremost in our minds … but i was not on the way to a combat unit … i was on the way to fort meade maryland … to await orders to flight school … i was now a lieutenant … a second lieutenant … again my experience meant nothing … i was on the lowest rung of the ladder and just by the virtue of my rank knew nothing … i was not too sure if i was going to like this officer thing or not … but hey … flight school was in my future …

… always have something to look forward to …

… always and have theme music too … but i had the nagging feeling that if i was an officer it could not mean that much … it was not important if it was me …

… seems like that is a curse …

… yes really …

… **in limbo** …

… i could say that there is not much to fort meade … but that would be an understatement …there is a big difference in the officer ranks as to the value of a person based solely on their rank … i arrived at the post just before christmas and took leave home … my family treated me as if being an officer as some sort of secret … it seemed they did not know how to treat this new kid on the block … that is the way i felt … my world changed with the commission … i out ranked every sergeant and warrant officer in the army … i did not parade that fact … as a matter i felt displaced from that fact …

… what fact …

… i felt estranged from my old life … the system of enlisted soldiers … as a specialist five with three overseas tours … one being viet nam … i had experience … i was among the pros … as a second lieutenant i was surrounded by others that had no experience what so ever …

… that plus the fact that i was only going to be there six months as i was awaiting orders to flight school … i was not considered for any assignment that required depth on the bench … i was assigned to a supply platoon … it had six enlisted men and six sergeants … and besides looking over a lot of property and world war two barracks that were empty … well it was not much to do … i was a little unsure of myself … therefore i was trying to get along to make the six months as pleasant as possible … but … and this is a big but … but the troops were radically different than the army security agency troops i was used to …

… how so …

… well they were not very motivated … they too knew they were all in a nothing job … it was as if we were in it together … kind of like the crew in the movie mister roberts … from boredom to tedium and back … there was another platoon and those guys were assigned to stoke the coal heaters in the building … that is all they did … can you imagine doing that for a couple of years in the army … i felt it was a misuse of manpower … the troops morale was really bad … i left them alone and let the sergeants give them assignments … which is the way it is supposed to be done … they would inventory property that had not moved in years … the count was the same each time … week after week … month after month …

… i had two feelings … i felt sorry for them and wanted to get to flight school … it was also the first time i had any dealings with the womens army corps … women were limited in the jobs they could do in the army … it was normally clerical or logistics … they were not even allowed into the intelligence field … how dull …

… i became frustrated and out of sorts about four months into the time there … i was depressed … no very depressed … it was the start of my adverse reaction to being an officer … i was fortunate to be an officer but i did not necessarily like it … i felt isolated and not part of the corps … after all i was a high school drop out and most of the lieutenants were college grads … i felt less than … but i got a reprieve and left meade after six months … i had no one to say good bye to … it was if i was never even there … i packed up my gear and headed in my corvette to fort wolters texas and the beginning of a school that was to have the greatest impact upon my military career …

… okay … let me get this straight … you went through o c s yet did not feel a part of the group … i mean with your experience and patches and badges you would have stood out a little at least … i mean you did have a year in viet nam …

… the thing is i was so lacking in staff ability … i was not well versed in writing … i mean my english experience was a story about being captured by gypsies … and tactical reports …

… yeah i recall that one …

… i was not ready for command … had i have been in an infantry unit i may have been given some training … but a supply platoon … i also knew not to try to stand out least someone find me out …

… find you out …

… yes i was in a position to bring attention to myself and i did not want to … i would have given up the commission for staff sergeant stripes at any time … i was a …

… duck out of water … do you not think that a lot of enlisted soldiers that become officers feel that way …

… everyone i ever met … but we also have an understanding of what it is to be a private and have no say in things … i was a private in turkey but i had a lot of say in the day to day operations … i kind of got spoiled …

… were you apprehensive about flight school …

… not really … it pulled me out of my blue funk and kicked in the mania …

… you had something to look forward to …

… exactly …

… you were saying you were off in your corvette …

… i loved that car … a lieutenant in a corvette … go figure … i was poor … i did not make much money … actually i made more money as a specialist five because i drew jump and proficiency pay … when you added it up it was more than a second lieutenant …

… you had a corvette …

… let me put it into perspective … the payments were just under one thirty a month …

… for a vette …

… hey it was sixty seven …

… off to texas …

… with the top down …

… i can see your enthusiasm even now …

… oh yeah i was going to be a pilot …

. allow me to digress … were you not required to write reports and have some paperwork in o c s … surely you had some staff work … they were not going to throw you out there with no staff training …

... oh i did well with that in o c s ... but i signed it all ... it was my work with my signature ... but at meade things were different ... i was writing work for others signature and felt i was not as polished as the other lieutenants with college ...

... i see your point ... what about flight school ... was there no need to write reports and the like there ...

... none what so ever ... it was filling out forms and logs ... we were there to learn to manipulate a helicopter ... the only thing that i was leary about was the math ... but i did well enough in o c s ... so i considered i could get through it ...

... obviously you did ...

... to fly ...

... i pulled into fort wolters in the little town on mineral wells texas and followed the signs to in processing ... always processing to do ... it was an all in one thing ... a packet to fill out and some pay data ... i would get an extra four eighty a month in temporary duty pay and an extra one twenty five for flight pay ... my pay more than doubled ... oh and there were dozens of corvettes in the parking lot ...

... after in processing i was sent to the supply room for an armload of books and manuals and flight suits ... i was also given a list of what to buy at the bookstore ... some gear and a cap ... an orange cap ... as that was the color of our flight ... each flight had a different color cap ...

... i stayed at the holiday inn for a few days ... i had little to do until i reported in on a monday to get our schedules ... i found out we were taken everywhere in buses ... it saved me a lot of gas ... i noticed three guys hanging around the pool ... they kept talking to others at the hotel about flight school and how great it was ... i thought they must have graduated ... but i could not figure out why they were still there ...

... later i saw them out processing ... they had busted out of the school ... a fate i did not wish to befall me ... i also thought that if i busted out i would keep my mouth shut about the experience ... then it hit me ... what i did not like about being an officer was the endless self promotion required to get a good efficiency report ... i knew little about efficiency reports and could not have cared less about what we referred to as the report card ... i will tell you right now the officer corps is the only culture that ninety percent of the members of the corps are above average … i would later learn that if you did not get a maxed out report card you were dead in the water … a ninety nine could kill your career … i thought it was just absolutely hokey …

… we assembled our class or rather our flight on a monday morning … i remember when i first in processed they had a form with a block to put our height at the top … now i understood why … we were divided into three sections and the tallest group … me included … would fly the h twenty three … it was an old korean war vintage aircraft made by hiller a defunct copter company … the other two flights were assigned the t h fifty five a hughes copter bought by the army to use for training in the primary course … fort wolters was the primary helicopter training center … we would be there four months and acquire at least one hundred hours of flight time … i realized the reason for the height assignments is when i sat in a t h fifty five … it was a short stubby little thing … it looked rickety … but i was not flying it … i was in the twenty three … the flight started off with two weeks of ground school … we learned about the functions of a hand computer used to define everything from fuel burn rates to time distance computations … we also learned the specifics of the h twenty three … after two weeks came the moment of truth … our first day at the flight line … i was really excited and ready to go … i did not know however if i would really like or take to the airmanship required for the course … those three guys at the pool kept coming into my head … i was bound and determined not to be like them …

… we met our instructors … i was to be trained by a civilian instructor … for the first fifty hours we had civilian instructors … they would teach us how not to kill ourselves … really … when i look back on it that about sums it up …

… i was briefed on what we would do that first day and i was lucky enough to get the first flight … i would fly to our training stage field … i was taught a little about the preflight … but did not soak too much of it in and i was concentrating on not messing up on the flight out … then we went through the start up procedures … soon we were taking off … once leveled off at about five hundred feet the instructor explained the manipulations of the controls … in our ground school we were taught about the cyclic … not called a stick as some are … was the directional control … he let me move the cyclic back and forth to experience the pitch and then i moved the cyclic from side to side and felt the effect of roll … next he had me place my feet on the pedals and feel the nose go from left to right known as the yaw access … i had experienced the three axis of maneuver … pitch roll and yaw … he took back the controls and we landed at the stage field which was a building a tower a refueling area and four short runways … he landed to a runway and moved to the far end … it was here he allowed me to manipulate the collective … the collective gives power and pitch to the rotor blades … as you increased the collective adding to the pitch of the blades you had to increase the throttle for more fuel and thus more power … he let me work the collective and while doing that he had me put my feet on the pedals … guarding the controls he then had me take the cyclic … i was to hover the copter … it was an effort in coordination … keep the aircraft over one spot with the cyclic … keep it three feet off the ground with the collective and throttle and keep it straight with the pedals … that was hovering …

… i went about ten feet into the air and tried to control the throttle to maintain a certain r p m of the engine … i swung wide and wild from one side to the other with the cyclic and spun halfway around with the pedals … i had hovered … and that is a loose interpretation … i had hovered for about two minutes and thought he was the bravest man i ever met … and he did not laugh … i was trying the best i could … i was then and there convinced i would never be able to hover the copter … i knew it was beyond my skills … he took control of the aircraft and i looked around … all the others at the stage field were doing the same thing … all over the place … he took me back to the stage house and let me out to go get a fellow student … i was wringing wet with sweat … the hover got me … he assured me i would eventually find what is called the hover button … the button he told me was more in my head than in coordination … i was like a school kid … in fact that is what i was … a kid in school … but i was in army flight school … and the executive officer from viet nam was right on target ... it was better to go through this as an officer than as a warrant officer candidate ...

... then it happened ... four days into the course and i picked the aircraft up to a three feet hover with the throttle and collective ... i kept it in one spot with the cyclic and kept the nose straight with the pedals ... i had hit the hover button ... i knew then that i was going to make it ... i was keeping up with the class ...

... one maneuver that got every ones attention was the autorotation ... you had to demonstrate proficiency in that task more than anything to be able to solo ... an autorotation is where you take power from the aircraft by retarding the throttle and reducing the collective to take all the pitch out of the blades and you start on your way down ... it is used to simulate an engine failure ... you keep a steady airspeed during the descent ... then you start a deceleration by bringing the nose back and slowing the aircraft by taking out the airspeed ... at about ten feet you level the aircraft and start pulling collective to slow the rate of descent ... but pulling the collective slows the rotation of the blades ... there is no go around ... you get one shot at this ... i remember the first one ... my legs were shaking ... nothing will save you more than a good autorotation ... in my career i probably did a thousand or more ...

... the rest of the time was spent honing our basic skills ... but there is another day i shall never forget ... i was at about the eleven hour level and my instructor told me to hover off the stage field lane and park in the refueling area ... he got out of the aircraft and walked away ... the tower called my number and i was told to take the lane ... i was about to solo ... i took the lane and took off ... i was to do three traffic patterns ... after i took off i turned to the right to the cross wind leg and kept on climbing to seven hundred feet ... i then turned right onto the downwind ... it was then i looked over to my left and no instructor ... hey ... i was in this thing by myself ... i can remember saying to myself ... just do not quit ... i was talking to the engine ... it kept running ...

... i did the three patterns and was soloed ... after we got back to the town on the bus ride i would be thrown in the pool ... it was tradition … i got back to my room that day soaking wet and feeling i had jumped another hurdle … this old high school dropout was keeping up …

… the first fifty hours brought me new confidence … i was seeing the end of the training with the civilians … soon i was at a different heliport with military instructor pilots … all of them viet nam vets … it was good to talk to them and hear about what it was like to go over there as an aviator …

… the class was now starting into the tactics portion of the course … it was not fighting tactics it was the tactical planning of things like formation flying … cross country navigation … night formation flying … night cross country and some low level flight … i loved the night portion of the flying … i became good at planning compass directions and gauging time and distance with the hand computer …

… i knew from my jump experience that you could see the ground at night and make out references a lot better than most people think … plus i learned to use a road map as well … i carried a road map of the tactical area … if you keep a steady compass direction it is easy to pick up roads and reference them to the map … the roads were on the tactical map as well … so what you do for each leg of the cross country is you plot check points on the maps and fly the flight plan … the system was not very sophisticated … but it was effective … i was taught basic procedures that would serve me well in the future …

… the last two months at fort wolters went by and we graduated from the primary course … a funny thing happened during those four months … we all came together as aviators … we had a common bond … i did not feel like an outsider … it was the first time since my first tour in viet nam … i referred to it as my first tour because i knew i was going back … now on to fort rucker and the real preparation for the war …

… were you surprised that you felt the way you did … the bond …

… yes … i was really surprised at myself … we were all in it together … it was a very primo skill … to fly … we were actually a sub culture of the army … but to our individual branches … the infantry the artillery the armor the engineers and so forth we were second class citizens …

    … how so …

    … each branch was a sub culture in itself … just as the special forces was a sub culture … this thinking had a marked effect on our careers …

    … again how so …

    … it is a little early in the story to get into that … we will address it more in the future … at this stage of the war and at this stage of the armys involvement in viet nam the need for officers was great … it was an automatic promotion to first lieutenant after a year and another year after that it was an automatic promotion to captain … we had some very young captains running around the army … some only twenty years old … as far as experience went in my flight class i was an old timer … at fort wolters i was an old guy at twenty two years of age … many were older than me being college grads before coming in the army … but as far as military experience i was one of a handful of viet nam vets … i was the only one in my flight with an intelligence background … that and the security clearance that went with it was to effect my career …

    … you seemed to have changed as to your thoughts about being an officer …

    … not really but being an officer allowed me to be a pilot … and it was a pilot i wanted to be …

... in the air now ...

... i got in my trusty vette and drove to fort rucker alabama ... the home of army aviation ... i entered my last six months of training ... again with the gear issue and a stack of books ... i had just put the stuff in my car and behold across the company grounds walked my commander from viet nam ... he had since been promoted to major and was in the fixed wing class ... i ran over to meet him and he was genuinely glad to see me ... now you have got to understand ... this made me feel uncomfortable ...

... why ...

... i was not used to having anyone look forward to seeing me ...

... ah ... i get it ...

... anyway ... back to the inprocessing... one of the books we were issued was the huey manual ... the u h one was the hallmark aircraft of viet nam and the first classes we were to go to was huey training ... the first aircraft we would fly at fort rucker was the huey ... that day will stick in my mind for life ... again i was the first to fly out of the heliport ... all of our instructors were warrant officers ... they were the backbone of army aviation ... again all of them were viet nam vets ...

... i climbed into the huey and strapped in ... we went through the start up procedures and then the moment of truth ... bring it to a hover ... ah ... but the huey was a turbine engine powered machine and the throttle was adjusted by a governor as you increased collective ... so i did not have to monkey with the throttle to bring it to a hover ... i brought it straight up to three feet ... kept it over one spot on the ground ... and kept the nose straight ... it was a smooth piece of machinery … i hovered out for takeoff and went into the air with more power than i could imagine … we had twenty five hours to get a handle on it and it was easy … we had a lot more emergency procedures to learn but the bookwork and the flying brought us even closer to nam …

… in a month i was a huey pilot and then on to instrument training … the key to instrument work is to be light on the controls … radical maneuvers will throw you off and make you over compensate with the controls …

… we were trained in aircraft we were not qualified in … the h thirteen … it was the same aircraft used in mash the t v show … i was in the army inventory from before the korean war … we were back to throttle control again as it was a piston engine … it was smoother than the aircraft we flew at wolters …

… instrument training is not easy … there is a lot to control at once and navigate and tune radios … the instructor was along for the ride … we did everything and the instructor would cover up instruments to have us fly with minimum reference …

… our classroom instruction consisted of instrument fundamentals and we spent time in the simulator which was a little blue box on a stand … but it did everything the h thirteen did … it was a good training devise for the unsophisticated training we were to get … and it was very unsophisticated … it was the basics … essentially it was enough to get us down safely if we were to punch into the clouds …

… i had a technique as to how to fly the instrument courses … it was a mob of aircraft out there … and i mean a mob … we would climb to an altitude and you had to keep that altitude to maintain separation … and the separation was three hundred feet … that means that if two aircraft were off one hundred fifty feet they could collide … all our turns were to the left as the instructor could see to clear us … my side of the copter was completely blocked in by panels … i could not see outside the aircraft at all … everything for me was on instruments …

… the greatest fear of an aviator is a post crash fire … and real close to that were mid air collisions … especially with low level operations …

… anyway the method i taught myself to navigate was to use the instrument charts like a map with the turns on the beacons as check points … a map is a representation of the earths surface as seen from above … without a map i am lousy and have no sense of direction …

… we did have a midair collision in our class and four were killed … two instructors and two of our classmates … it got our attention as to clearing our maneuvers before we turned into them … somehow the two aircraft got off enough in altitude to collide …

… i got through instrument training without a hitch … of that i was very proud … then came the fun part … gunnery training …

… the tactical training started and we were to fly gunships and shoot rockets and machine guns from the hueys … it was all with an instructor pilot … but it was fun to dive from altitude and strafe the targets … or we would come in at tree top level … the training was only a week and then we moved on to the training that would prepare us for missions in viet nam …

… our classes were now all about tactics and the roles of the branches of the army … we learned the mission of the infantry the cavalry and the artillery … we spent a lot of time on cavalry operations … the air cavalry was the premier fighting force of the war … the cav got into it more than any other aviation entity …

… during our next to last week in training we went on a field problem … we lived in tents and operated in a totally tactical environment … we flew formation flights with a crew of two students … no instructors to help us out … we were all on our own … of course the tactical missions were not beyond our skill levels … but we were happy to be crews none the less …

… then on to the last week of all classroom work with no test at the end … all but one of us received orders to viet nam …

… and i was about to get married …

… huh …

… yeah … during leave before i went to fort wolters i ran in to a family friend … we dated and got serious … she came down to fort rucker to stay with me over christmas … she had an eight year old daughter …

… she was older than you …

… yeah … no matter … but my family got all up in arms about it … to tell you the truth no matter who i dated they got up in arms about it … i did not think much of it but my aunt was enraged … it seems i was not doing what she wanted me to and continued with the relationship … actually i was conducting my life against her wishes and she would not allow that to stand …

… another huh …

… my family was afraid of my aunt … she had to have it her way or else … she would cuss and fume and raise a stink about anything that did not please her and the rest of the family went along with it … all but one … me …

… so what did you do that was so horrible to bring that on …

… well i call it living in the stink …

… in the stick …

… no not stick … stink … in the stink of dysfunctional lifestyles … i had been away from it for so long i was not susceptible to it anymore … temper tantrums were the way to maintain control in the family … they all did it except my cousin … he just went along to get along … after all my aunt was his mother … what else could he do …

… i guess the next question is … what did you do …

… i put off the wedding to try to make piece … i tried … but when my aunt laid down the law and told me i could not get married until i got back from viet nam i told her we were going ahead with it … that did it …

… one of the questions my mother had about the marriage was that if i got killed in viet nam would my wife get the station wagon … good grief … i had traded the vet in for a more family friendly car …

… lovely …

… yeah … that is about all you can say … what a lovely mess …

… i left it like that … but my aunt forbid anyone in the family to communicate with me again … and they abided by that …

… surely they eventually got in contact with you …

… nope … did not see my mother for thirty five years when she died … she wanted nothing to do with my wife and me …

… indeed … good grief …

… we were married for fifteen days and i was off to viet nam almost two years to the day from when i left … it was march of sixty nine …

… back to the repo depot at fort dix …

… not this time … on to travis air force base in california … from there the short route to bien hoa air base … the same place i left from my first tour … i was in country again …

… were you manic or depressed …

… i was in a depressed state as i had just gotten married and i was back to the same place i left … i could look across the airfield and see the s e a huts we lived in and worked out of in sixty seven … the brigade was gone … it had moved up north … a dark gloom overtook me … it did not realize it would happen … i thought having one tour under my belt would make the second a better experience … one tour had nothing to do with the other … except the leadership was much better on the first tour … more of that as we get into the second tour …

… so you are saying the leadership was worse on your second tour … how so …

… viet nam became a requirement for careerists … it was if they had to get it on their records … get their ticket punched so to say … they were using the troops for their own benefit … the troops were there to promote their agenda … again this will come out as we go along …

… how did you come to know of these careerists …

… they showed up late in the war … they were just arriving in sixty nine and seventy … where had they been since sixty five …

… sorry i do not mean to get ahead of you …

… no … that is all right … the two biggest things that brought the whole thing down around the administrations head … viet nam that is

… was the fact that we were shipping draftees in country … and the idea that we could gauge our winning by body counts … this will all come out as we go along …

… it sucks …

… tet is the buddist new year … and in january of sixty eight the whole of south viet nam erupted on tet … the n v a even got into the u s embassy …

… n v a …

… north vietnamese army … the viet cong were on their last legs … attrition had taken them out … we had so many troops on the ground that the v c could not maneuver as they had done before … that and the agenda of the north which was to hand a blow to the allied forces and fritter away the viet cong and make the war an n v a stand … and it worked … it was a morale objective … boost the morale of the viet cong and lower the morale of the allies and it worked … after tet the war was not the same … the south was demoralized and we were now in a fight that put us against better trained and better equipped troops … but everytime the n v a met us in force we beat them … but to them that was not the fight … the fight was for the hearts and minds of the american people … by that i mean the american public started to get turned off by the war … if we were winning how could the n v a get into the embassy … the allied commander in viet nam was reassigned to become chief of staff of the army …

… so we had a new commander whose training was in armor on the central european plain …

… just as you had been taught in o c s …

… exactly …

… from the air base at bien hoa i was taken to a repo depot in long binh to await assignment … i rode i a bus with screening on the windows and an m p escort with machine guns just as on the first tour

… i had hoped to be assigned to the first aviation brigade but soon found out it was the first cavalry division … the premier airmobile division … four of us from our flight school class went to the cav as we referred to it … we were flown north to ahn khe where the cav had made its home for four years … it was just the remnants of the division there along with the one seventy third airborne brigade … my old first tour unit … i went over to the club to talk to the folks over there … you would have thought that with a combat patch on from the brigade i would have met with someone to welcome me back … but because i had a cav patch on the other sleeve i was not welcome … what in the world was that all about i thought to myself … i said hello to a major and he would not even acknowledge me … just stared right through me and then walked away … i noticed he had no combat patch on as it was his first tour … let me stop here for a minute … i am sensitive but i am trying to make a broader point … the way military leaders make up for their lack of ability is to act like a hard guy … a tough guy … it was something you had to put up with … screaming officers are not the way to get things done and keep up morale … but they were not there for morale … they were there for self promotion …

… so i went back to the cav side of the fence and within a few days had my assignment to the eleventh aviation group …

… when asked to list what unit i wanted to go to i put down the ninth cavalry … the first squadron of the ninth cavalry was the premier flying unit in all of viet nam … the cav was the best and the first of the ninth was the best of the best … but it was not to be … upon arriving at the eleventh group headquarters i found out why i was not assigned to the ninth cavalry … i had a top secret special intelligence security clearance from my past duties with the army security agency … it was because of that clearance that i was to be assigned to the eleventh general support aviation company and then to the platoon known as project left bank … i did not know it but my clearance was about to haunt me …

… i was dropped off at the orderly room of the company and was met by the operations officer … in no time i was shown to a s e a hut that would be my home … the other members of project left bank were quick to come over and meet the new guy … everyone … commissioned officers and warrant officers had been members of the army security agency as enlisted soldiers … i had something in common with the platoon …

… it would be two weeks until i was to meet the company commander and that was just in passing on the flight line … if he outranked you he did not wish to bother with you … i had never received any kind of an in briefing by the commander the executive officer or the operations officer … after awhile i felt i was just there and serving not much of a purpose what so ever … it was fine with me when i look back on it … i kept to myself and waited for clearance to fly with the platoon … until that time came i flew single ship missions in support of the division command and staff … i got to fly over quite a bit of our tactical operations area … which because of our mobility with five hundred twenty two helicopters was very expansive …

… after awhile i was cleared by the division intelligence staff to fly project left bank … it all seemed a big secret … but before i flew my first mission i was given a briefing at the division g two which was the intelligence staff … the briefing consisted of an outline of our tactical area … the mission of the division and then … and then … well … and then a briefing as to the enemy we were fighting … i just stood there and listened as this major who was the g two plans officer talked about the north vietnamese regiments we were in combat with … it was the two seventy second … the two seventy third and the two seventy sixth … i just stood and stared at the map as i heard the numbers of the same units i had listened in on and identified and fixed their locations on the map with the brigade on my first tour … it had been three years since i arrived on my first tour and we were still fighting the same units … only now they were listed as north vietnamese army units … what is the difference i asked myself … on my first tour i learned a lot about the intelligence business and i was the only one in the platoon with a former tour in country …

… counting the time the brigade was there before i arrived on my first tour … we had been fighting the same war in the same manner for four years … i did not say much about what i was thinking as i had not been assigned to any project left bank flights and wanted to get to know the mission … i had seen the aircraft on the flight line with a long antennae sticking out in front … little did i know how much my first tour would come in handy …

… my first mission came up and i was ready to go … there were only three aircraft like ours in the division … i thought it was cool to be in left bank … came the first mission and off we went north of the camp at phouc vinh … it was explained to me that the operators in the back … two crew members from the radio research unit of the division … would search the radio frequencies for vietnamese voice or morse code traffic … we would then turn the aircraft in the direction of the radio … once we had a compass direction on the radio frequency we would lay the aircraft over and look straight down to find our position over the ground … then we would fly to another spot and find the compass direction from there … two compass directions and we had a cut … three or more and we had a fix … sound familiar … this was the ultra secret special mission project left bank … the exact thing i did on my first tour except it was from an aircraft … well i was a bit disappointed but took to the mission real well … in essence i got a handle on it pretty quick … being the new kid on the block i just flew for a few weeks until i was made the assistant operations officer in the company … i was still flying with the project but had operations duties as well … and then the operations officer was selected as an aide de camp for the assistant division commander and i found myself the operations officer … again the commander was not around and during the two months he had left on his tour he came in to the operations one time … i had one major problem and that was i was the lowest ranking commissioned officer in the company but i had the number two job … it was like pulling teeth to get anything out of the platoon leaders … but after awhile they figured out i was not getting much help … and lightened up a bit on the captain lieutenant thing … i guessed that i was doing okay as the commander never said anything … one thing i did not care about was the efficiency report … the good old report card … it never crossed my mind to care about it … the last time i heard from the commander was when he called me from bien hoa air base and told me there was something he forgot and would i take care of it … and then he told me that he had given me a ninety five on my report card … out of a hundred that was …

… in comes the new commander … again no word from him one way or the other … and to my recollection he never once came in to the operations building … this is what i mean about the leadership on my second tour … as long as we … the junior officers ran it okay … the commander had nothing to do with us …

… then one day i was told by the project left bank platoon leader that i was to be assigned to the division g two and they needed someone with my clearance to serve as the g two target officer … whatever that was … because of all of this intelligence stuff coming my way i requested a transfer from the infantry to military intelligence branch … within a week or two a message came back that i could not be transferred as there were no efficiency reports in my file … no report cards what so ever and i was within three months of being promoted to captain … essentially i had no career … all my time as a lieutenant was an absolute waste of time …

… getting hit by rockets and mortars and shot at in the air did not make me as angry and as manic as the fact that i was of so little value that no one would even evaluate me as required … it was inappropriate for the rater not to render a report card … the value was not for me to work specifically for an efficiency report … that was playing politics … but the fact that i was forgotten … well that set me off … i was on the verge of rage … and it was because i was a reserve officer not regular army and not very well educated … but i was on the division intelligence staff …

… i had a hard time fighting the depression but seemed to stay in the rage … i did not lash out at anyone … i just kept it inside …

… *tell me about the rocket and mortar attacks* …

… one forty three sticks in my mind … in the three hundred and fifty days of my second tour we got hit with rockets and mortars one hundred forty three times … or there about as i may have missed a day or two on the calendar … i hated them …

… *any close* …

… yes a few very close … one rocket hit and threw dirt over us but the shrapnel flew over head … some i slept through …

... slept through ...

… yeah … we made bunkers out of our huts and only a direct hit would have gotten us …

... and shot at ...

… yeah with small arms fire and fifty caliber … we were not hit … close … but not hit … early into my second tour i decided that getting the crew back alive every day was my premier duty … early into my second tour … especially after the g two briefing i decided that the protestors back home may have had a point …

… i was at tan son nhut for some meeting at the third radio research group … i ran into my old commander from my first tour … he had developed a real bad attitude … i found that to be common among the second and third tour people … anyway … there was this young soldier sitting on a bench outside of the base operations … i asked him where he was headed … he told me to the twenty fifth infantry division in chu chi … he had been there for two days and no one had picked him up or made any plans to … even though chu chi was about an hour out of our way back to phouc vinh we took him to his unit … seems he was a draftee and had just come back from r and r … his unit made no provisions to get him transportation … he was a draftee and that could have been the reason he was forgotten about … or it was just more lousy leadership …

… then it dawned on me … why was a draftee over here … at no time was our national security at stake … it took four years plus of the war for me to grasp that and understand why the public was so up in arms about viet nam … then came the worst morale breaker for the whole in country population … it was called vietnamesezation … which is not really a word … but what ever … the president was pulling out units … when that happens who wants to fight … the only difference from the unit next to yours is that they are being pulled out and you are not … not good for an incentive for the troops to fight … and the troops were responding very negatively to the policy of vietnamizing the war …

… even though i was on the g two staff i still flew with the project and flew other missions with the company … i still lived there until after christmas of sixty nine … one night i was in the rack reading and i heard a thud … the thud was familiar … it was an american grenade … i had heard many on my first tour … were they among us with american munitions … i got up and looked out of the hut and heard screams coming from the hut just across from mine … four sergeants had been hit with a grenade … it did not take long for us to figure out that someone in the company had thrown a grenade into the hut … none of the four sergeants was killed but all four were in serious condition … we had a fragging in the company … we had a murderer among us … we never found out who it was … people speculated that the fragger had been out to get one of the sergeants and the other three were just there …

… i did not consider that … i thought some drugged up trooper just wanted to get as many as he could with one grenade … it kept us very alert after that … our fragging incident made national news … it was usually bad leadership in the field that brought on those kind of attacks … but an aviation unit on a secure base made no sense …

… my job at the g two was to locate major enemy units … principally the three units i was briefed on at the g two plans … i also plotted arc lights … that was the name of b fifty two strikes and sky spots … the name for bombing runs by f four fighters … i got to blow up a lot of jungle during my five months at the g two …

… i will say this … i really respected my boss … a lieutenant colonel on his second tour and the g two himself … who later became a four star general and supreme allied commander of n a t o … i was promoted to captain and was among a lot of other captains on the staff … we all came from company sized units and all got along very well … my first tour in country counted for something … i proved to adapt to the staff work very well … i simmered down and could even laugh at some of the silliness of our prolonged war … to give you an example … the command in saigon was big on body count … every time a unit made contact with the n v a they would send in a body count … they never recovered much in the line of actual bodies claiming the n v a carried them off … plus they never had much in the way of captured equipment … sometimes the claims were outlandish … but each battalion had a running score on body count and they all tried to outdo the other …

… i also kept a map that was for the tallying of the christians and lions … the lions were the n v a and the christians were our troops … thus the contacts were addressed in that form and a dead american became a christian statistic … and a dead n v a a lion … when i look back … well … it was revolting and my boss knew i hated the stats on that map … but every general that visited the division received my briefing on the christians and lions … another point of the war … the troops had been reduced to stats … the war had devolved into a numbers game to the staff in washington … it was the way to keep score … the president said it was a good week in viet nam as only one hundred thirteen soldiers had been killed … i thought that it was a very bad week for those hundred thirteen …

… a night before i was to leave the g two awarded me a bronze star … i left the cavaly division with a load of medals … the distinguished flying cross … eight air medals … and the bronze star … i thought i had salvaged something out of the year and even had a few report cards in my file … none of them were one hundreds … which meant i was in the bottom ten percent … remember the top ninety percent were all above average …

… off i went to the repo depot at long binh … in a day or two i was on a big iron bird to home and the new marriage … we had met in hawaii for six days half way through my tour … so i had been married for three hundred sixth six days and had been together for twenty one … we had to get to know each other all over again … and i was a different person from the lieutenant that left a year before … i was twenty three …

… *what did you get out of viet nam* …

… i do not understand …

… *what did you come away with* …

… the main object of war is to stay alive … of the three aircraft we lost one and the crew of four … we had no guns on the aircraft so we had no door gunners … the aircraft was shot down by a fifty caliber machine gun … i understand it went in inverted as the rotor mast was shot off …

… is not the object of a war to win it …

… in the pentagon yes … but on the field of battle it is the right of every soldier to stay alive … do not get this mixed up with any action other than taking the fight to the enemy … but when engaging the enemy on the ground as the infantry did you get behind something to protect yourself … you advance in quick bursts to lessen your exposure … you can also back off and call in artillery … it was always prudent to have artillery on call … why get into a one on one if you can just blow them up … that is what we did from our aircraft … we called in artillery … when we took fire we called it in … but you had to be careful of a trap …

… how so …

… the n v a would fire at you and then go to ground in holes … we would call in artillery and then if you went down on the deck to see if you hit them they would jump out of their holes and shoot you down … it was an ambush trick … we never fell for it … besides you either hit them or not … if the artillery wanted a body count we would just say a number of suspected n v a killed … by the time it got to battalion it was a confirmed count … we did not care … frankly what did it matter …

… we did however come across bunker complexes and small encampments and called artillery in on them … we could see the damage from the air and reported it as so many bunkers destroyed or so many huts leveled … again we did not fall into the ambush trap …

… an ambush sounds more like the infantry …

… yeah … they had to deal with it too … they would make contact and a few n v a would run away from them … if the inexperienced infantry leader would run after them with his troops they would get into an ambush … a trap set by the n v a … and no matter how much training they still fell for it … we kind of got off track … your question was what did i get out of viet nam …

… yeah … let us get back to that …

… i came away from my first our with the idea that we were making a difference … i came away from my second tour thinking that the only career you can have as an officer was a future of shameless self promotion …

… shameless … that is pretty harsh do you not think …

… no … what i saw after nineteen seventy was an army falling apart … i am glad we did not get into something during the time we went from a draftee army to an all volunteer force …

… you wanted an all volunteer force …

… quite the contrary … i wanted it to be a draftee army … by seventy three when the brass learned that the country would not stand for using draftees for a war that was not for national security the pentagon went to an all volunteer force … it began in seventy three and we had no draftees after seventy five … but we had the left overs of the one hundred thousand program …

… what was that …

… it was a program by the defense department that allowed the enlisting of one hundred thousand troops that were really not qualified …

… how not qualified …

… most were illiterate … many were not of the intelligence required for basic military skills … it was more than one hundred thousand … it was closer to four hundred thousand before the pentagon got smart and stopped the program … the army was rife with poor caliber troops in an effort to tell the public that the volunteer army was working … our n a t o forces were packed with them … i am not faulting the soldiers but i do fault the brass that considered their tactic worthy … between the careerists and the lacking troops the mid seventies were a mess …

… so … i guess i am back to my original question … what did you get out of all this …

… hey … i was a captain with a family … i was back at fort wolters texas and in a pretty good situation … i was the executive officer of a warrant officer candidate company … but déjà vu … i had to deal with majors that were just the dregs … i knew as a captain at that time

… well … i had an active duty assignment … i was a reserve officer on active duty … like thousands of viet nam vets i was just in the army … the goodies went to the regular army … and i could see why … just think about how … they called us christmas help … just think how much we would have clogged up the promotion system …. the main purpose of an officer was to get promoted no matter what … but the officers that were former enlisted men and women … well … we did not think like that … the object was to do your duty whatever the assignment …

… you sound as though you were bitter …

… no not bitter … educated … i was educated as who to stay away from … anyway on to wolters …

... more majors ...

... before you get into it too far can you give me the low down on this majors thing ... sounds like you did not get on with majors ...

... not really ... i just ran into some that were a little hard to take ...

... for instance ...

... well ... where do i start ... ah ... let me go back to viet nam ... there was this major that was the deputy g two ... one afternoon he called all the captains in the g two ... there was about six or seven of us ... anyway ... he calls us together and tells us that the success of the war rests on the shoulders of the company grade officers ... lieutenants and captains .... of course being a major he never thought of his role in the war ... that mindset came from some of the senior officers ... generals ... complaining about the poor quality of officers ... the war was going downhill fast and the president was just trying to get us out of it by turning it over to the vietnamese ... the senior staff had to blame the mess on someone ... it was as if the c e o of a company was blaming the clerks for the company going broke ... the major was on his first tour in seventy and we were on our second and one of us on his third ...

... okay back to the major thing at fort wolters ... when i processed in i asked to go to a warrant officer candidate company ... i wanted to get with the troops ... i was assigned as the executive officer ... the company was commanded by a major ... i had to sign for all the property which is the responsibility of the commander but as a major he did not want to bother with such a thing ... then i found out the reason for it ... these majors wanted to get their command time in ...

… command was the premier responsibility of an officer and these majors had none … to get a report card you had to be in a position for at least sixty days and that is what was going on … they would put a major in for sixty days and then rotate another in … i asked when i was going to get a command … the question fell on deaf ears … i was to just administer the company and let a major come in every sixth days … again the fact of being a reserve officer raised its ugly head as all the commanders were regular army …

… a staff job came open and i leapt at the chance … i was to be the education officer at the flight schools center safety office … safety is a big challenge in aviation … i was to write a column for the post newspaper … produce a weekly safety t v show and serve on accident investigation boards … we averaged five accidents a month which was good as we had a student body of over thirteen hundred taking flight training … students prang aircraft …

... how about the marriage ...

… oh we were doing fine … i was learning as i went along as to being the dad of a ten year old … my daughter and i got along great …

… and for my wife and i … well we had a lot of social functions to go to … and one of our goals was to save money … like all couples …

... how long were you in the safety office ...

… a year and a half … i enjoyed it … in was administrative work and by virtue of that my writing skills improved … i even started to write a book about slavery … a novel …

... you knew a lot about slavery ...

… no i just made stuff up … it is funny i read only nonfiction but like to write fiction … except for this …

... yeah ... how did this come about ...

… a little more later but i was asked to write a bio after having another book published … but that is real late in the tale …

... okay on to wolters ...

… as i said i served at center safety for about a year and a half and then got the job as post protocol officer … a guy i was in viet nam with was in the job and asked me if i would like to take over … he was going to be the commander of a warrant officer candidate company ... yeah ... he was regular army ...

... how long did you stay at the protocol office ...

... well i had no orders to go anywhere ... oh ... there was one thing that happened ...

... how so ...

... the army was being cut back as viet nam was really wound down as of seventy two ... they were putting officers back into the reserves from active duty ... it was called a reduction in force ... or as we called it a rif ... and the first round of rifs came in the summer of seventy two ... all the reserve captains were edgy over it ... i however was not hit by it and made it through the first rif ... so i thought ... i was not doing too bad if i did not get caught up in it ... by that time i was on my way to fort huachuca arizona for the officers advanced course ... it was a captains course of nine months and i was fortunate to get it ... by then i had successfully transferred to military intelligence ... i was about to compete with officers that had masters and p h ds ... needless to say i was somewhat anxious ...

... so how were you doing mentally ...

... the assignments i had at wolters were real low stress ... but any bump in stress could bring on outbursts ... my wife and daughter just attributed it to my personality ... and i did as well ... but it was something i could not control ... i think that time in my life was relatively calm ... at least for me ... i was under a lot of stress in california ...

... california ...

... yeah ... i forgot to tell you about that ... soon after going to the center safety office i was sent to what we called safety school ... it was taught at the university of southern california ...

... u s c ... the army sent you to u s c ...

... yes indeed ... it was a program taught in the aerospace safety and management department ... we over did a semester ... we were really loaded up ... eight hours a day five days a week ... for me it was the moment of truth ...

... how did you get in as a high school dropout ...

… that is what i am about to get to … i went over to the department and knew i was about to be found out and sent back to wolters …

… did they know at wolters … did they know you were a high school dropout …

… yeah sure … but they sent me anyway … so off i went and when i got there i was told to go to the registrars office … ah … unmasked at last … but the administration merely handed me a piece of paper showing i had been registered and that was it …

… when i finished the program i was an alumnus of u s c and a graduate … i no longer needed a high school diploma … so when i got to advanced course i could say i was a u s c graduate … but i was still a little apprehensive … this would be college level work for a year … little did i know i had a leg up on the military intelligence branch only classmates as i was from the infantry and all of our exercises were from the viewpoint of the infantry … for the first time that i can remember … of all my commissioned time … i was a little ahead of the power curve … it was not until a lot later in my career was i to realize how valuable the both u c s and the advanced course would be …

… how long had you been commissioned by now …

… going on four years …

… and you felt you were behind the power curve all that time …

… indeed … i always felt that i was going to be caught being over my head … i felt that way as a private … why would i not feel that way as a captain …

… i see your point … you alluded raging … did you understand what set off the rages …

… no i did not even think it was the stress … i would rage during stressful times but it was always under a controlled environment …

… controlled environment …

… yeah … i raged mostly at home or in the car alone … i remember i went into a rage over the car not starting with my daughter in the car … i felt bad about it … i felt out of control when i would let go … i never let go at work except to go out to the car and scream … i know it sounds crazy …

... not really ... what you are telling me is that even though you raged you were in control ...

... does sound crazy ... i was in control of getting out of control ...

... did you have this going on at the advanced course at huachuca ...

... no not really ... the advanced course was a real low stress environment ... except for some of my classmates ...

... how is that ...

... out of a class of about sixty ... oh ... i would say about fifteen of them felt the course was beneath them ...

... i do not understand ...

... we had a lot of masters degrees in the course and they felt the academics were less than their education ... they were superior to the course ...

... a quarter of the class ...

... at least ...

... but you said you got through with no trouble ...

... except for one part of the instruction ... and that was on computers ... i mean how much knowledge was there as to computers in seventy two and three ... what we had back then were selectric word processors ... i forget the brand ... and then we had the punch cards for sorting ... but what the class was about was an h g wells look into the future ... i passed the test okay but i wished i would have done better ...

... another area i had trouble with were the writing assignments ... we were taught english classes and i had to brush up on my writing skills ... but i got the hang of it and did all right there ... computers and writing were my biggest challenges ... we also had to take additional classes ... we could either take two college courses or take a course known as national security management from the industrial college of the armed forces ... i took that program and one extra course on china ... i was sort of an over achiever in the advanced course ... but i always had the idea in my head that i would have to catch up ... so when i graduated in seventy three i was both an advanced course grad and a graduate of the industrial college of the armed forces … i was catching up … but it did me no good …

… what i thought was a benefit to my future by transferring to military intelligence was not to be … i thought i was doing all right as i got the transfer to military intelligence … what the branch was doing was transferring in as many as possible so they could be used for the reduction in force coming in seventy three …

… you got caught up in the rif …

… yeah … it was the last one for reserve officers … i had made it through the last two but this one got me … right after the advanced course and right after i arrived at fort bragg and right after i bought a home … i was so upset by it i got out and became a civilian for the first time in ten years … i was twenty seven …

… what did you do …

… i went to job fairs set up by companies to hire rif officers … back then it meant something to have military experience … now it does not mean a thing … more of that later …

… where were the job fairs …

… downtown fayetteville just outside fort bragg … it did not take me long to get a job … but i erred …

… you erred …

… i erred in that i took the first thing that came along … i was that insecure … plus it was a sales job … albeit a salaried sales job … but i am not a people person …

… could have fooled me …

… no really i am not … i try to be pleasant but i really am not the sales type … anyway i went to new york for training and then was send to the dallas office …

… what did you sell …

… children s sleepwear to major buyers … but the dallas mess was not good for me …

… dallas mess …

… yes the sales manager in the dallas office was a lot of trouble for the company … and they sent me there as a leavening factor … now i was under a lot of pressure … i had a family and just left the security of the military …

… how could it be secure if they dumped you …

… oh i could have stayed on as a sergeant … but i wanted to try civilian life … i could always join the reserves and make extra cash with them … anyway … i had sold a home in fayetteville and bought one in dallas … i had begun a new job that did not seem too secure for me and the pay … well … when i put it all together was pretty lousy …

… so … one day while sitting outside a movie theater with my wife and daughter i thought of the time i would be wasting …

… wasting time i do not get it …

… i had ten years in the army and only needed ten more to qualify for retirement … i told them i thought it would be a good idea to go back in as a sergeant and work up from there … they agreed and i enlisted within the week …

… so you were a civilian for how long …

… about four months maybe five … it was the best thing i could have done … it taught me some valuable lessons … i learned the bottom line trait of civilian companies … at no time did i feel a part of anything …

… unlike a military assignment …

… right … and to top it all off the sales manager of the company was an f four pilot that just happened to get out as viet nam was starting up … i did not think a whole lot of him and i think he sensed it … but when i told them i was leaving the sales manager and his assistant told me i had been doing a real good job …

… i was in a very deep state of mania that lasted for about the first three months of me being back in the army …

… did you not have a hard time going from a captain to a sergeant …

… not really as i had been enlisted before … plus i went into the infantry as i knew enlisted promotions would be better than intelligence … and we went right back to fort bragg and the best division in the free world … the eighty second airborne division …

... i have heard of them ... that good huh ...

... they are the first to jump in ... that good indeed ... when i got to the division i knew what was going to happen ... i was assigned to an infantry unit for one day and then was called up to the division headquarters to talk to the g three about working for him ... when i met him i knew he was going to be a general officer he was that sharp ... he wanted me on the staff ... when i got settled in and got to know the other sergeants i came to find out that a lot of them had been rif officers ... the g three was padding his staff with former officers ... i thought it was a very bright thing to do ... i worked in the force development office for about six months and then what i considered the best job for a sergeant on the g three staff came open ... i was assigned to the adjacent air base ... pope air force base ... there i would do all the load planning not only for the division but for the corps ... eighteenth airborne corps that is ... it was a twenty four seven operation so i had some weird hours ... but i developed into a great load planner as my aviation experience was plus ... it kicked me into a mania that lasted for nineteen months ... i went through jumpmaster school and jumped all the time ... i had a great boss ... he was great to work with and he really trusted me ... soon he was leaving me alone down at the operations and when he was hurt in a parachute accident i was left down there alone as the g three had a lot of confidence in me ...

... let me explain my mania at this stage in my life ... it was positive mania ... while working at the airlift job i finished a college program ... it was sort of a diploma mill and it accepted my military credits toward the degree ... with u s c the industrial college of the armed forces and the advanced course i only needed a few courses to finish a degree in political science ... i also finished the sergeants advanced course in infantry and armor ...

... busy guy ...

... i was really hitting my stride ...

... so you went from the rif to being on staff at the g three of the eighty second ... pretty good ... you know what you never finished the story about the military intelligence rif ...

… i have that and a better rif story for you …

… go ahead …

… well the reason the military intelligence branch took in so many transferees was that the officers management knew that the rif was coming they had to provide a certain percentage of officers based on branch population …

… so they used the branch transfers for the rif and kept the military intelligence officers …

… absolutely correct … but here is what the pentagon did in seventy five … the army was still needing to cut back its company grade officers … but they were out of reservists … they could not touch the regular army officers as when they got promoted they were given a guarantee of time … if you made captain you were given six years tenure … it was a law … not to worry … the pentagon convinced congress to rescind the law and rif regular army captains … so the guarantee of tenure was reneged on and the army threw out thousands of regular army officers … it was one of the most craven things i saw the army do during all my years of service … that is how bad the quality of general officers were during the seventies … i am not talking about the division commanders or even the three stars at corps command … it was the politicos at the pentagon …

… the preponderance of the officers rif were viet nam vets … the army was ridding itself of the viet nam experience … i think i got more upset at that rif than my own … simply stated the captains caught up in the seventy five rif were lied to and the senior staff and congress thought nothing of it …

… in late seventy five i volunteered for duty in vicenza italy … i was to do the same duty i had at fort bragg and i was to work for another squared away major … see … the majors are getting better …

... italy and the big break ...

... a lot of units bill themselves as the best in the army and that is what the parachute battalion in vicenza did ... the battalion had no real world missions and very poor training resources ... the battalion was a subsidiary to the command which primary mission was nuclear surety ... we controlled the nucs in italy greece and turkey ... in other words the nucs were in those countries but could not be used by anyone but us ...

... i never heard of those countries having nucs ...

... we did not give them tactical nucs ... but the weapons were stationed in the countries ... the command was the southern european task force ... it was not a combat command ... with the exception of the battalion the command was a staff function ... i eventually ended up in the same job as i had at bragg except i was the sergeant in charge of the training office ... i did all the day to day administration and two army majors one air force major and an italian lieutenant colonel were the staff officers assigned there ... so i had to keep up with them ... it was not high stress at all ... aside from sending troops to training we had very little to do with nucs and a lot to do with n a t o exercises and the battalion ...

... it was a good job for me as i got to travel to germany and other n a t o bases in italy ... however after the eighty second airborne division it was a little bit of a let down ...

... we lived good though ... my family and me ... the high school was real good for my daughter and it was fun to travel around the city ... we took a trip to france and my daughter got to go to rome ... that is a funny story ... my daughter was in high school for about three days after arriving and she came home with a permission slip to go to rome with the school ... back home it would be a trip to the farm or some factory ... in italy it was to go to rome ... it is that kind of learning experience you get in assignments like that ... my wife had a good job in the bank on post ... as a staff sergeant i was one of the lowest ranking sergeants on the staff ... i was hoping to make sergeant first class ... but really did not trust the system ...

... why is that ... did you not do a good enough job to get promoted ...

... i did a good job and had great report cards ... it was that the last time the pentagon staff touched my records i got caught up in the rif ...

... ah ... did you get promoted ...

... well i got promoted beyond my wildest dreams ...

... how so ...

... i was in the office one day and this major came over and asked me if i had been an aviator before ... he noticed the wings on my chest and had talked to my boss about me ... well ... he had a piece of paper with him ... it was a message to all commands personnel offices ... it seems in the army s infinite wisdom with the rifs year after year ... well ... they put out too many aviators and could not fill the cockpits so to say ... essentially the army was short aviators ... so the pentagon was soliciting the field commands for any former aviator that would like to come back on flight status as a warrant officer ...

... warrant officer ... you mentioned them before ... what exactly is a warrant officer ...

... a warrant officer is an officer that has a chosen field of expertise ... in my case an aviator ... but they are in intelligence ... logistics ... personnel ... and they become the go to guys and gals for the commanders that want in depth information in their field ... warrant officers are the best kept secret in the army ...

... well ... as soon as i heard that i applied ... i do not think an hour went by until i had my application in to the warrant officer branch ...

... it took about two months for them to send my application up before a board ... but i got it and got a reassignment to the eighty second ... things were really looking up ... i knew i would at least retire as a warrant officer ... thus i could retire an officer rather than a staff sergeant ...

... this was a very fulfilling time in my life and i would not have gotten the promotion if i had not gone through the aerospace safety and management program at u s c and had not been an advanced course graduate which was the kicker ... as i was an advanced course graduate i would not have to go through the warrant officer advanced course ... i also had a reserve commission ... as a captain ...

... whoa ... how can you be a sergeant and a commissioned officer at the same time ...

... it was called dual component ... i was an active duty sergeant and a captain in the reserves ... and to enhance my promotion possibilities for major in the reserves i took the marine corps command and staff college ...

... marine corps ...

... yeah did it for the fun of it ... something a little different ...

... mania ...

... you got it ...

... we packed up in seventy seven and moved from italy to fort bragg ... with fourteen years in the army i had hit my stride ... i was an aviator and paratrooper in the best division in the free world ...

... jumping and flying ...

... did you have a hard time adapting ...

... not at all ... the rank of a warrant officer is between sergeants and commissioned officers ... i fit in real well ... i was assigned as the safety officer in the general support company of the eighty second aviation battalion ... and just as i got there we were scheduled for an inspection ... i was good with staff work by then and we passed with kudos ... it was a challenge for me but because of the inspection i got a real handle on the company and my job ...

... i did not fly much until after the inspection and i had to go through all of the training to establish myself as a part of the flyers in the company ... i was flying the huey again ... and i was the safety officer of the most accident prone company in the division ...

... why is that ...

... most accidents ... we called them mishaps ... most of the accidents in the division happened on single ship administrative missions ... and all we flew was the division command and staff on single ship administrative missions ... i took to the training with verve ... i was going to prove myself and do so in the eighty second ...

... the major commanding the company was someone i had worked with before on my tour as a sergeant ... as a matter of fact because i was in the airlift business i worked with all the units on fort bragg ... i had a lot of contacts both officers and sergeants ... that came in handy ...

... i was also jumping and served as one of the battalion s jumpmasters ... jumpmasters are responsible for the safe executions of the jumps ... and i did it for free ...

. for free ... how is that ... how can you do something for free in the army ...

... at that time you could only draw one hazardous duty pay and i chose flight pay as it was three times higher than jump pay ...

... i see your point ...

... i started flying missions with a guy that flew the assistant division commander ... a brigadier general ... one star ... i really enjoyed that as you got to get involved in all sorts of things ... another benefit was we had plenty of down time waiting for the general ...

... how is that a benefit ...

... i had time to work on my marine corps staff college ... i remember standing in formation and receiving the diploma ... i had officers coming up to me and asking if that was the same as the army course ... my answer was yes ... i had the staff training of a major and lieutenant colonel ... i really enhanced my standing in the battalion ...

... kind of an over achiever were you not ... mania ...

... you know this was probably the sanest period of my life ... i would not call it mania ... no ... i was really tuned in to the mission of the company and the battalion and the division and enhanced my training ...

... my experience with flying the general got me in good with the command and staff and when the generals pilot was reassigned overseas i got the job of flying the general ...

... so you were not the safety officer anymore ...

... no ... i did both ...

... a little busy ...

. i was ... but i handled it ... i flew the general for about a year and then decided i would make a move to flying gunships ... cobras ... we were having a reorganization and we were getting an attack helicopter company ... twenty one cobras ... i asked to go to cobra transition ... and the commander i got was the best major in the army ... he was head and shoulders above any major i had ever worked for ... and the lieutenant colonel commanding the battalion was also the best light colonel i had ever served with ...

... there was only one hitch ...

... what was that ...

… the battalion commander was a born again christian and i was getting back to my jewish roots … oy vay …

... jewish roots ... you are italian ...

… allow me to enlighten you … outside of israel venice italy has the highest percentage of jews … the highest per capita …

... huh ... never knew that ...

… hitler shipped thousands of italian jews off to the camps …

... so back to your jewish roots ...

… on my fathers side …

... but you said you did not know your father ...

… the lineage came from my grandmother langiones family … i had a motive also … i wanted to relate to the israelis … i got my training at the synagogue on bragg … i even got circumcised … the whole magilah as they say … i enjoyed that spiritual part of my life …

... circumcised ... ouch ...

… nah … after you get past the third day all is well … hey … i had a customized batszim …

… if you can call it that … however … my wife was not to keen on it …

... cause any problems ...

… a little bit but we worked through it … anyway … it was the time my daughter was applying to colleges and she settled upon a school in philadelphia … we took her up and our young lady went in to the dorm and was on her own … i look back on it and realize it was good for her … we kept a close watch of course … but i knew she would do all right … and she did … she was able to finish her second year of school when i got my orders to germany …

… the tour with the eighty second was second to none or so i thought … i had heard of the eleventh armored cavalry regiment and the unit was stationed in fulda … the fulda gap was important as almost all of our field problems were based on defending the fulda gap when the russians and east germans breached the east west border … the regiment was the first line of defense … this would be my first time in an assignment other than an airborne or air mobile unit … it was an armored unit … things just kept getting better …

... it is the Russians over there ...

... i was on a real roll when i got the assignment ... to get it i wrote the regiment and asked to be assigned there ... had i not done that it would have been the luck of the draw and i did not want that ...

... i went ahead of my wife and daughter ... my daughter decided to come along as because of her age she was still a dependant ... i do not like that term ... the word ... dependant ... but that is what the pentagon calls the family members ...

... i noticed over the last few chapters you have gone to the first person singular ...

... i am getting close to when my illness started to take over ... it was subtle at first ... but really ... the best years of my life until two thousand four were spent in fulda ... a lot of it had to do with the location and the language ... i am after all half german ...

... when i arrived in germany at rhine main air base in frankfurt i knew i was starting on a great adventure ...

... was there music playing in your head ... theme music ...

... but of course ...

... what made this tour of duty so special ... and you seemed to know that from the get go ...

... i did ... i was coming off an assignment that allowed me to grow as a warrant officer and i had been at the top of my game in flying and jumping ... i even went through the eighty second free fall course ... i had ninety nine jumps ... why not a hundred ... heck anybody can get a hundred ... not really it just turned out that way ... when i left jump status i had ninety nine and it was all good ... i had cheated death and defied gravity as an air force colonel used to say ...

... i was awarded master parachutist wings which were the highest you can go ... i was looking forward to learning about the armored business and on the ride from the air base to fulda i believed i was back home in pennsylvania ... the countryside looked the same ... it was nineteen eighty and i had seventeen years in the army ... when i had eighteen years in i would be guaranteed retirement ... this was something i knew my wife worried about ... we talked about it when i took the warrant ... i had hoped i was not setting myself up for another rif ... but by germany i had it made which did take some stress off of us ...

... the post in fulda had been an old barracks of the german army ... there were nazi eagles on the building but the swastika had been sandblasted off ... it was a small post as there were only two battalions stationed there ... only in the cavalry the battalions were referred to as squadrons ... the city of fulda was beautiful ... it was old europe and some building went back to the dark ages ... it was the home of saint benefacious ... whoever he was ... i was much more interested in the sites in germany than i was in italy ... oh ... i enjoyed the sites in italy ... the visits to venice and verona ... just driving the autostrada was an adventure ... but germany ... now germany was the center of the prussian empire ... it had the history of the goths and was the site of so many second world war battles ... i started to read a lot about the war in europe on the central european plain ... it was patton ... it was bradley ... it was eisenhower ...

... i started a collection of books on army divisions and read the history of the war from the landings in france to v e day ... i was in a historians hog heaven ...

... soon after arriving in fulda i was given a briefing as to the mission ... we were smack up against the east west german border ... the west germans and the regiment patrolled the western side and the east germans and the russians patrolled the east ... there was a fence line that ran from the baltic to the austrian border ... actually the border fence and fortifications ran from the baltic to the black sea ... there may have been east germans on the border but the russians commanded it ... it was the russians we were poised against ... and the border was divided into three sectors … the sectors were coincidental with our squadrons … the center squadron was in the center at fulda along with the air squadron … to the north in bad hersfeld was the third squadron with its own portion of the border and the second squadron was in bad kissengen with a border sector that went south to our sister unit the second armored cavalry regiment … they patrolled southern germany and the czechs …

… what i learned about our mission is that we and we alone patrolled the border and only a chosen few were allowed the responsibility of being qualified to fly all three border sectors … if another aviation unit wanted to fly the border they had to stop in fulda and pick up one of our pilots … i wanted to be one of those tri border qualified pilots … and no map work … the ingress routes and egress routes plus the whole border sector had to be memorized … it would take about a hundred hours of flying to get the three border sectors down …

… as luck would have it i was assigned to the general support company called a troop … it was the air support troop and i was assigned the safety officer job … we fly the command and staff … and i was assigned as a co pilot with the regimental commanders pilot … we had a colonel commanding and he was referred to as the r c o … regimental commanding officer … he would be the best colonel i ever worked with … he impressed upon us that we worked together … form the privates to the lieutenant colonels … he was a tactics genius and he knew more about the armor equipment than anyone i ever knew …

… i flew most of my flight time for the first three months with the r c o and learned the border … at first you have to reference it to the map … you have to memorize the map and then relate it to the ground you are covering … the border was by no means a straight line and you had to know every twist and turn … with the r c o i learned the terrain between fulda and frankfurt as we would fly to the corps headquarters … in three months i knew more of the terrain than most of the pilots that were there for years …

… there is a difference between flying real missions and training missions … real missions like flying the r c o and his staff required on time takeoffs and good navigation … it also requires that flights be made in adverse weather … the weather conditions we were legal to fly in was a hundred feet ceiling and a quarter of a mile visibility … that is really close to nothing … i used the term legal to mean i was regulated as to the weather restrictions … the weather conditions we often flew in were lower than instrument minimums … i flew fifty feet above obstacles and rooftops … i got complaints about this … it was tactical flying and i had to navigate low level which is a lot harder than at altitude … besides if the population complained i would ask which is better american helicopters of russian tanks …

… my wife got a job at the bank on post and my daughter got a job in the post exchange … we made the most money we ever had and we able to travel all over europe … we took trips to italy and france and holland and austria … all over the place … but one of the best trips we took … no … the best trip i ever took was to berlin … we visited the same general i had flown at bragg … he was now commanding the berlin brigade … we went into the east several times … even went to the airport to look at the russian aircraft … it was a very spartan international airport compared to the free world …

… we were just driving around the city on the east side and came across a huge statue of lenin … it was in karl marx platz … we stopped and had a cup of coffee … then we were off to the russian world war two veterans memorial … it was beautiful … fine inlays of ceramics and gold and silver … there was no graffiti … in fact we saw no graffiti in all of east berlin … not even on the communist side of the wall …

… next we went to the tomb of the unknown soldier … i saluted the guards and went inside … it too was inlayed with gold … i had to travel in uniform … but we did get to follow a group of russian tourists … we just followed their tour bus around and saw the sites with them … we went to a shopping center and people walked up to look at our car … it was a big station wagon and i just opened the doors and let them sit inside … it was a lot bigger and certainly a better product than their little zils …

... we went to lunch in a hotel and ran into the same group of russian tourists ... they acknowledged us but did not come over to shake hands or talk to us ... i looked at them and felt bad for them that they did not have what we had in the west ...

... i was not their enemy ... my job in europe was to keep the peace ... not start a war ... the officers and sergeants that wanted to start a war wanted to do so for the perceived glory of it all ... the viet nam vets wanted nothing with that ... and a slave stood behind the conqueror holding over his head a golden crown whispering in his ear a warning ... all glory is fleeting ... i love that ... it says so much for those that have never heard a shot fired in anger ...

... the russians were on vacation just like we were ... i can actually say i never met a russian i did not like ...

... oh i have got to tell you this ... this has to do with my playing theme music in my head ... when we first went to berlin he had to get travel orders to cross from west germany into the east ... we started out from fulda late in the afternoon and by the time we got to the crossing point to go into east germany it was dark and raining ... we got our orders stamped by the staff at the western border site ... then we were to go into the east and report to the border guard ... it was a scene out of a cold war movie ... there was a cement block wall with rusted barbed wire curled on the top ... a shack with a dim light was to the right as we pulled in and a guard stood to our left ... i stopped the car ... it was raining and the lights around the guard post were a dull yellow ... i went up to the guard and saluted ... i handed him my orders and he looked at me and in perfect english said ... hey man do you want to buy a belt buckle ... thus my spy movie scenario was ruined ... i told him thanks but i already had a russian belt buckle ...

... we made the trip to west berlin not being able to see much in the rainy dark of night ... what impressed me was the dimly lit houses ... it was as if their electricy was at fifty percent ... on the way back we traveled in the daylight and got to see the countryside ...

... thus was our introduction to the communist side ... the warsaw pact side ... i was very happy to be on the n a t o side ...

… a good part about being the r c os pilot was flying senators and congressmen around … we always took them out on the border … we had this favorite spot on the border to the north … it was called the halfway house … the border cut right through the middle of this farmers house … he never went into the eastern side … he had it walled off … we were not allowed to talk to the east german or russian border guards but after awhile seeing the same people over and over we kind of relaxed that role … i would talk to the sergeant at the border post near the halfway house … he was just a soldier on his post … but it was interesting the way the guard posts were set up … not to defend against the west but to restrict movement from the east … anyone trying to escape from east to west was to be shot … it was very tightly controlled with a fence and land mines …

… one day we flew out to visit a section of the border fence that had been flooded and washed down … two young east german soldiers were standing right in front of me … they had a booklet with insignia in it and were trying to identify my jumps wings on my cap … they were not sure if they had it right so the one guy showed me the picture in the book and i nodded that he was correct in his identification …

i also got to fly formation with a russian hoplight helicopter … i flew in a wing formation with him … he on the east side of the border fence and me on the west … stuff like this went on all the time … we were relaxed … the politicos were the ones that kept up the tension …

. last flying story … we were on a tactical operation with two divisions and us involved … there was a turkish general commanding the n a t o southeast command … he was to see the war game on his day tour of the field site … well the weather was bad and he was being driven around and was not a happy camper … well he came to our field site and we were to show him the disposition of our tanks … the weather was bad but not that bad … as he approached the aircraft i greeted him in turkish … he lit up with a smile and the flight came off without a hitch … the blackhorse regiment looked very good that day … i used to grandstand like that all the time …

… when i first arrived in germany i got my car stuck in the mud at our apartment … this farmer from across the street got his tractor and towed me out … he was talking to our landlady and she interpreted … as i listened to the farmer talk i could understand about half of what he said … he sounded like my grandfather in pennsylvania … i decided then and there i was going to get a handle on german … i was functional in italian and became real adept at german over the years i was there … i even interpreted for the commander and staff … again it gave me a great grandstanding opportunity …

… i had one opportunity that i did not feel i could grandstand …

... what was that ... no theme music ...

… no none what so ever … the pope was visiting fulda … yeah that pope … and i was asked to interpret for his staff as they were to receive a briefing about our mission on the border … i considered it and thought i might be in a little over my head … so i suggested my daughter do it … she would do much better …

... she spoke italian ...

… yes … during her second year in fulda she went to florence to attend the michaelangelo institute for language and culture … in six months she was fluent in italian … she was a much better candidate for the briefing …

… it went off really well … the staff gave her presents and got a real kick out of this young girl briefing them on our n a t o mission … she did a lot of adventurous things … i neglected to tell you we went through the free fall class together at bragg and we jumped together … we did a lot of stuff together … her mother said i married her just to have someone to play with …

... how many years did you serve in germany ...

… three … the best three years in the army … it was a real challenge for an aviator … especially with the weather … the fresh aviators … the youngsters just out of flight school got a lot of valuable experience in those three years … unlike the pilots assigned to stateside units … the germany pilots were head and shoulders over the statesiders …

... so how were you doing ...head wise that is ...

… i was in a manic state most of the time … i enjoyed the fact that i was in such responsible positions and really liked being the r c os pilot … but it was time to move on … i was assigned to fort campbell to the one hundred and first airborne division … it was the air assault division and i was going to the cobra instructor pilot course enroute …

... a screaming eagle ...

... i went on to fort rucker from germany ... i attended the instructor pilot course before signing in to fort campbell kentucky ... i had but two hundred fifty hours in the cobra and found the course ... at first ... a challenge ... but about three weeks into it my experience started to show through and i knew i would make it ... it was not without raging mania ... not out in the open but in my head ... in the evenings after class and during the weekends i would often lie down for hours and just stare into nothingness ... i put myself under more pressure for the course than i needed to ... i felt as if the world was on my shoulders to finish it successfully ... i was way overboard on the situation ... i had completed the psychological operations officer s course and the warrant officer senior course while in germany ... after all this was just another course ... but the weight of things was starting to get to me ...

... get to you ... how so ...

... i felt i was being graded all the time ... graded in everything i did ... it was draining ...

... what were you being graded on ...

... everything ... it is a bit hard to explain ... i ... well ... it was not as if i felt i was being watched ... it was as if i would be taken to task for everything ... could i be good enough ...

... yet you had just come back from a very successful experience in germany ...

... stateside is different ... there is a certain carefulness in the states ... all the i s dotted and the t s crossed ...

... i get the meaning ... more rules ...

… more dumb rules … in the course i spent as much time on the paperwork and bookwork as i did flying … but my experience pulled me through … what i had to fight was the newer inexperienced students that had all the new books … the new tactics memorized … half the tactics were a lot of silliness that would not work anyway …

… for instance …

… a good example was firing antitank missiles from a hovering position … when you are hovering you have no movement except within the realm of the hover … when you are flying you can maneuver and avoid being hit … but the tacticians … who never heard a shot fired in anger … the tacticians had this idea that we were to fight like tanks … move no faster than the tanks …

… i soon settled in and played their game and memorized all that stupidity … i was bound and determined to teach tactical sense when i got to fort campbell … after six weeks i finished the course and went to state college pennsylvania to pick up my wife … she was staying with our daughter who was by then at penn state … when i got there a letter was waiting for me … it seems i had made major in the reserves and my orders for the promotion were waiting for me …

… off we went to fort campbell and the one hundred first airborne division air assault … the screaming eagles as the division was known … but it was an airborne division and my decision to go there … i would be an instructor pilot in the armys most sophisticated aircraft the cobra … the battalion i was assigned to was an all attack helicopter unit … there were sixty three cobras assigned to the unit … plenty of work for me to do …

… we got ourselves situated by buying a house in one day … it was brand new and settled in a cul de sac … i was enthused about the assignment … however …

… ah … a however …

… i was still feeling the strain of being graded all the time … i had to go through a long check out process not only for flight and maneuver but for the local regulations on the forts training area … even though the post was fort campbell kentucky the greater part of the training area was in tennessee … and that is where we bought our home … clarksville tennessee … we got settled in with our household goods from both germany and what had been in storage at fort bragg …

… i was one of the most high time aviators in the battalion and was one of two viet nam vets that was an instructor pilot … the first thing i noticed was that there was a difference … no … a big difference between the young pilots at fort campbell and the young plots with germany under their belt …

… i take it the germany experienced pilots had it over the stateside guys …

… by a long shot …

… it was not until i was appointed the company standards officer … there were instructor pilots there with more instructor time but i could do the staff work and we had a big inspection on the way … a few of the other instructors did not like it … but i was also the highest ranking instructor … we passed the inspection no sweat and i was getting into the groove after about a year there and then i was offered a staff position at the division headquarters … it was a ground assignment and i would not be flying … right after we went up to see our daughter graduate from penn state i started the assignment in warrant officer management …

… i had started the army command and general staff college the year before and that was noticed … the staff job was to manage the careers and training of eight hundred thirty five warrant officers on the post … it was right up my alley … but again the feeling of not doing well enough cropped up in my head … i would say that the year i worked at the staff g one was a rewarding experience but i felt i was not good enough and would be caught and labeled a phony … and really no warrant officer on the division staff had my military education … i was born for staff work … but the gnawing lack of confidence got to me … after a year in the job i decided to retire … there we several reasons … i wanted to go out on a good assignment which i was in … i wanted to retire from an airborne unit … and i wanted to get away before i got caught … looking back it seems like a horrible situation i put myself into but it was my mind set at the time

… it was the beginning stages of my serious mental problems … i was starting down the road to a bipolar nightmare … although i showed the symptoms earlier … even in childhood … the illness was taking hold and really encroaching upon my psyche … but it would do it slowly and for awhile make my life … well you will see …

... the hunt for a deep pocket ...

... i made sure i had a good job before i retired ... at least i thought it was a good job ... we ... the three of us as our daughter had joined us ... the three of us were headed to dallas texas where i was to investigate aircraft accidents for a law firm ... out of all the resumes they screened i was the one chosen to work in the law firms aviation department ... i was brought up in the military since seventeen and was shielded from the culture of the civilian tribes ... oh i had that small stint with the clothing firm twelve years hence but this was different ... we were not talking about a few paltry bucks for sales of girls sleepwear ... this was millions of dollars in lawsuits ... hey ... what did i know ... really i knew from nothing about tort law and law suits and bottom feeding lawyers ...

... i got a rude awaking and a real education in no time ... the first saturday i worked there a jetliner crashed at the dallas fort worth airport ... my first mission was to discover the cause of the accident ... i knew from my past experience in the military that the cause of an accident was a myriad of chance happenings collected together by events that came together at that precise moment to create the crash ... this would not be easy especially since the information would not be made public for some time ... but ... what one can do is follow all the leads from people in the investigation business that run their mouths to the press ... there is something about a camera and a microphone that allures people ... i fell into that in a big way ... but it was to set into motion a chapter in my life that was the most rewarding ...

... what i did was put together the information in the papers that filtered through in the weeks to come ... the stories about structural damage and weather and the flight crew and more ... taken separately were not very informative but when you put it all together it told a story and there were plenty of human interest stories to be told about the hundred or so victims ...

... what i learned was that the information about the accident does no good unless you have clients and clients is what we were after ... lawyers are by law not allowed to solicit victims of mishaps or malpractice or other damages done to them that would fall under tort law ... by the way tort means a thing wronged ...

... i was going to ask that ... i have heard the word applied a lot but never looked it up ... crime reporters do not get into much civil law ...

... i had to figure out how to get clients without contacting the families directly ... this was a lay down as far as a suit went ...

... a lay down ...

... yeah ... it was a big payoff at the end thus the more clients you had the better off you would be ... we also had an advantage in the firm ... it was well known as a tort factory and the aviation department was well known for winning cases ... we did get a lot of clients and they were mostly by referral ... an attorney would take the case and then lay it off on us to work it up ... there were quite a few victims from a sorority ... we ended up with referrals from them ...

... what was the cause of the accident ... did you ever get the whole story ...

... yes ... it was weather related ... a micro burst threw the aircraft into the ground on short final ... the pilots were somewhat at fault as they missed a weather report ... that was indefensible ... so the recoveries came through and in the meantime we were on to several other mishaps ...

... it was interesting how greedy people got over the death of a loved one ...

... over the death of a loved one ...

... yes ... i worked this accident where this twenty one year old kid went flying with a guy that was not qualified to fly the aircraft they took for a spin ... the aircraft stalled and they were both killed ... we took the case on behalf of the parents of the kid ... they saw big numbers in their future and the loss of their son took on a whole new meaning … they eventually were awarded seven hundred fifty thousand … they split it and got divorced … i bet you the money did not last for more than a year … we got two hundred fifty thousand of it … one third always came to us … we probably put less than forty hours on the case before the case was settled … another lay down …

… were most of the cases that easy …

… oh no … some were easy to dump …

… how so …

… when i got there we had a bunch of cases back logged … and some were real dogs … one case these guys stole the aircraft back from maintenance and took off in it with no oil in the engine … on another case a drug dealer took off on an airstrip out in the middle of nowhere and crashed on takeoff … cash was strewn all over the place … the d e a and i were both going over the wreckage at the same time … i worked the case of a famous person lighting the aircraft aflame from the rear … we did not take that either …

… one of the best cases we had was a case in canada of a charter aircraft crashing at lake gander on takeoff … it was filled with one hundred first airborne troops … i went to fort campbell on that one … i briefed some of the staff on what lawyers did in these cases … i found even the colonels to be very naïve … they could not put together the crash and the windfall of money it would present to the law firms … the ones i knew could not believe i was involved in such a thing …

… one thing that got me was that i sold out too cheap and was making the same amount of money whether i made a bundle for the firm or not and i did work up quite a few crashes that paid a lot … but my primary job was to find clients …

… was the canada crash a lay down …

… oh yes … big time … i went to canada to sit on the mishap inquiry board and the whole truth came out … they were overloaded and could not develop one hundred percent power on one engine and did not use all the runway … the aircraft just mushed in at the end of the runway … had i not retired i would have been on that mission … now whether i would have been on that particular flight i do not know

… the local t v news did a story on it … the aviation lawyer and i were interviewed … after the interview some of the lawyers came by and said i did a good job … it struck me that until then they must have thought i was stupid as i was not a lawyer …

… know this … if a lawyer is in the room … that lawyer is the smartest one in the room … he will tell you that … since working in that law firm the only lawyers i can stand to be in the room with are all ladies … with the exception of military lawyers … i mean that … by the time i got out of there i had the impression that all lawyers were flaming … if you catch my drift …

… i catch your drift ... where did you go ...

… before i tell you that let me tell you what i was doing for fun … remember me telling you that i loved to watch movies on t v … you know watch the late show … well now i had a chance to be in the movies … there was a film school in dallas … it was called the film lab and i decided to check it out …

… it was owned and run by a movie star … as soon as i started classes i knew it was what i wanted to do … i was about to learn to perform before a camera … it is not an easy technique to learn but it is one of the only classes it took that you can see your improvement week to week …

… give me an example ...

… okay … a famous actor once said the key to success in acting is to know your lines … show up on time … and stay in frame …

… in frame ...

… yes … always before they start shooting know what the blocking is so you do not get out of frame … ask the cameraman and you will get it right every time …

… got any others ...

… if you are interested …

… please ... go ahead ...

… try not to blink … and do not blink in close ups especially …

... why not ...

… it makes you look weak … also in close ups always look at only one eye of the person you are addressing lines to … if you try to look at both eyes your eyes will move back and forth and it is real distracting …

… i will have to look for that … but it sounds right …

… so these are the things you learn and practice … i always found it weird that people would just say i am going to be an actor … with no training … just think they can go off and be an actor … also what i found out is a lot of actors are afraid of auditions … which to me is the fun part … you will not get any jobs if you are an actor that does not audition …

… so you took to auditioning … i guess you had to …

… oh i went over the top on my auditions … the reason i did that is the director knows that the actor can be brought down but if the audition is weak than the director may feel the actor cannot be brought up to the scene … it always pays to go over the top …

… did not the directors have you read lines …

… sometimes but i always asked to do a bit where i would not have to read off a script … i have a forty second audition that is a real draw … it will really draw the director in … it leaves them wanting more … which is what you want …

… so did you audition much …

… every chance i got … i even auditioned for parts that were not right for me …

… why do that …

… because that director may have another project and remember me … besides it is a numbers game … the more auditions you go to the more chances you have of getting parts … now dallas is not a big market for paying jobs … i got roles in a popular t v series … even had a few lines … it was my first job and i was thrilled … i got a few commercials and then i hit … i got a lead in an independent film … i was to play a native american in a slasher film …

… okay … what is a slasher film …

… it is a horror film in which all the principle actors are killed off one by one … except that is the staring girl and guy … i had third billing so i knew before i read the script i was going to die … we filmed it in waco … i was the last one killed and it was with a flaming arrow to the chest … good ending …

… right after that i got another role as a drug dealer in a story based … well loosely based on a true story … it was the worst movie i ever made … it was so bad it even won an award for being bad … but it got produced and distributed … it was a bit of a cult classic for awhile …

… *you seemed to have really enjoyed making movies … going to the film lab and all …*

… the law firm was developing into a dread … i kept feeling i was going to be found out … i was so insecure i even asked for a cut in pay because i felt i was not doing my job very well …

… *what … i have never heard of anyone asking for a cut in pay …*

… looking back it was like advertizing i was not worth anything … that must have been the message i sent to the firm … i knew i had to get out of there …

… but the film classes made me come alive … i was living in a nightmare of being depressed at work and then being up at the film lab … performing on film was something i could do … i thought it was the best thing i could do … if i would have been in los angeles or new york city i probably would have quit work to act … but in dallas there were no parts to think of … really i got most of the roles that came around … i was forty but could look thirty or fifty … i looked menacing on film and that was a benefit … i played an oil baron … a bouncer … a drug dealer … an indian … you see the pattern … i was not the leading man type … let me tell you this … character actors work more than leading men … i never wanted to be the lead name in a movie … you know why …

… *tell me …*

… if the movie bombs the lead gets the blame … who wants to take the blame for what might have been bad direction or bad editing or just a lousy story to begin with …

… *i see what you mean … you said … or a least i think you did that you left the law firm …*

… that is a funny story in itself … i got hired by the dallas police department and told i would be joining my academy class in about a month … so i gave three weeks notice … not they could have replaced me in three weeks and for twenty nine thousand a year …

… twenty nine grand a year … that was all you were making …

… yeah … and i did not even think i was worth that …

… incredible …

… self worth was not my strong suit at the time …

… so,,, i gave three weeks notice and two days later the owner of the law firm called me in and fired me … as it turns out … he did that with everyone that quit … several people quit and walked out and he would call them on the phone at home and fire them … i thought he was one of the most pompous people i ever met and i met some real head cases in the military …

… so you just waited for the academy to start …

…. no i worked at temp jobs until the class started … i had no faith in being in the class … everything by then was a shadow of reality …

… shadow of reality … what do you mean by that …

… i figured if it was something good happening to me i did not deserve it and if something bad happened to me it was punishment …

… you mean like being damned for your sins …

… not sins … i was being damned for just being …

… it sounds as if you were close to suicide …

… i thought of myself a coward because i did not commit suicide … i thought if i was braver i would have left my family better off … but i just could not do it …

… did you ever tell anyone about this …

… yes … you … now …

... the police ...

... joining the dallas police department was an escape ... an escape from people of whom which i was frightened ...

... frightened ... who frightened you ...

... i knew that getting fired from a civil service job was much harder than from the law firm ... i walked into the office everyday thinking i would be fired ...

... very insecure ...

... yeah ... let us talk about insecurity ... i think it comes with bipolar ... when mania sets in i thought i was not as vulnerable as i did when i was level or depressed ... i bring up being found out ... it was a constant for me ... actually it was a relief to quit and be done with the job ...

... yet you were unemployed ... you could have run out of money ...

... i had my retirement and my wife worked ... i know i placed a lot of responsibility on her and it was not fair ... this was my first unemployed period and it too scared me ... i was in fear employed and very insecure unemployed ... it was a double edged sword ... i was in a constant state of mixed emotions ... when i tried to explain this i do not feel i characterize it very well ... i did not understand it fully ...

... did you try to get help ...

... no ... i thought i could think my way out of it ... i would sit and stare and brood a lot ... it was a condition i was in that would not let me think of myself as damaged ... it was as if those around me were causing it ... i blamed everybody ... it had to be them ... it could not be me … it was a reason i joined the police department … but let us start with the academy …

… back to school …

… it was seventeen weeks … i thrived and even was voted class president … but again my insecurities were cropping up in my psyche … my head swam in the idea that i would not make it … i only had trouble with one test and that was the burglary instruction … it was my lowest test score … but the rest were in the nineties … really i over reacted to that one test … i did well with the physical training … the army training came out in the physical tests …

… like what … what subjects …

… self defense … hand cuffing … a physical training tests … pushups … sit ups … you know what i mean … i was the oldest guy in the class … we had study groups and would meet on sunday afternoons to go over the weeks material … it helped and we only lost one student during the academy … there was a broad range of education … i was not considered as having a degree because my b a was british … the army was okay with it but not the department … thus i was determined to get a degree in criminal justice …

… being the president i gave the graduation speech and then we were off to our assignments and field training … i was assigned to the oak cliff area of dallas … it was mostly minority neighborhoods … there was a lot of crime in the poor and rather well to do sections of oak cliff … most of it had to do with drugs …

… i was in a training program that taught us on the street procedures for seven weeks on three shifts … after that you were to come back to the original trainer and finish a three week period of being graded as though you were on your own … twenty four weeks of training … it was very stressful and we were on probation and could be let go at anytime … i was back to the feeling of being fired everyday …

… that soon into the job …

… i believed the main purpose of the supervisors was to get rid of people …

… after all that training … just get rid of people … seems like a waste …

… it was but we only lost one in training … and i think it was unfair the way that was handled … anyway … learning the street procedures was a matter of following a standards manual and even the older officers had to go to the book once in awhile … i had no trouble learning the procedures … if i went through a scenario once or twice i had it down …

… *what do you mean scenario* …

… everything from finding a stolen car to a drunk driver … drunk drivers were a real pain … the field sobriety test and taking them down to the jail for a breathalyzer test … drunk drivers took you off the street for quite awhile … that was another thing … all we did was go from priority one call to priority one call …

… *and what would that be* …

… say an armed robbery … a shooting … a murder … a rape … we were stacked up with those calls all day or night long depending upon the shift you were on … and dead bodies … i worked so many dead bodies on training … after training the dispatcher used to save the bodies for me as i knew the procedures …

… *murders … you have many of those* …

… i worked four in one weekend … oak cliff was a cops paradise … and during training i learned that the shift did not matter … we got just as involved on the day shift as the night shifts … except the night shifts gave me an atmosphere for the theme music in my head … you see i was not a cop i was an actor playing a cop … at least that is how i felt about it …

… *what about your acting* …

… oh … i continued with the film classes and got a good part in a film . the one i told you about where i played the native american … while in training i had week ends off and i got to use my comp time to make the film as my trainer was taking off … training became fun after awhile … when i was in my mania that is … i was learning the call procedures and was very good at reports writing … i was also getting to go to court and that experience enhanced my reports writing … i had one desk sergeant at the jail that told me he liked reading my reports as i wrote with style … i guess he liked my style …

... give me an idea what you are talking about ...

... you would start out the report with the call information ... who what when where ... the usual stuff ... but i would put the past record of the arrestee in the report and it added a little meat to the thing ... the defense attorneys have been swayed to plead out the cases instead of go to trial ... and i was very articulate in the courtroom ... my experience at the law firm helped ... plus i found the defense attorneys to be lacking ... sometimes i felt sorry for the hook ...

... the hook ...

... that is what we called a crook ... and we used the term hinky if something did not look right ... like pulling over a guy in an alleyway behind a twenty four hour pawn shop with six v c rs in the back seat ... that is hinky ... that was typical ... i had six felony arrests in one traffic stop one time ...

... traffic stops is where all the action was ... no drivers license no registration no insurance the guy did not even know his own name ... he is going to jail ... and when you figured out who he was you can bet he had warrants on him ... it was amazing the amount of people that had warrants on them ... and stolen cars ... i was always falling into a recovered stolen ... i would just get behind a car and punch the tag in the computer and it would pop stolen ... i had four recovered stolens on one traffic stop ...

... how was that ...

... this guy needed help evicting a renter and we ... my partner and i ... were told to go with him to make sure the people left ... well we get to the house and the renters are pulling out of the driveway ... i ran the tags and they came back with outdated plates ... he pulled back in the driveway ... i told him not to get out of the car ... on the computer was the registration for a sports car like he was driving and the v i n was listed ... i remembered the last four numbers of the v i n when i walked up to the car and the numbers did not match the numbers of the car ... so i went back and ran the v i n of the car he was driving and it popped stolen ... when we checked three other vehicles on the property they all came back stolen ... thus four stolens in one traffic stop ...

… i was doing real well and getting all sorts of overtime and was getting time off to go to school … i overloaded myself with courses to finish as soon as i could … plus i became somewhat proficient in sign language and got fifty bucks extra per month for that … rolling right along … and then we got a new chief … as soon as i met the guy i did not trust him … i nailed him as a boozer right off the bat …

… bad juju …

… very bad juju … let me tell you a little about the politics of the dallas police department … we had a very famous former new york yankee in dallas and we were not allowed to arrest him no matter how drunk he was behind the wheel … it even extended to his sons who were being pulled over all the time … also we could not arrest any football players … i did however arrest a globetrotter for outstanding warrants and cocaine possession … it was a sad tale …

… did you get a lot of drug arrests …

… yes … but you have to go through procedure and have a good reason for contact …

… a reason for contact …

… it is a step by step procedure … follow along … let us say this guy is pulling out of a known dope house or apartment complex and he fails to signal his turn … i pull him over … the traffic violation is the reason for contact … now i am betting he has dope on him … but i take it slow … first i get back up … another officer on the call … even if i have to wait awhile i do so … so the other officer arrives and i go up to the car … i ask him or her for a drivers license … she does not have one … so i just keep going but i know she is going down for what is known as jail traffic … but i proceed … again bingo … no registration nor proof of insurance … i get her out of the car and tell her to stand with her hands on the hood … i look around in the car …

… do you not have to have a warrant to do that …

… no under the case law of belton versus new york i am allowed to look at the places where a weapon may be stashed … i can open the glove compartment if in fact it is not locked … if a suitcase is on the back seat i can search it if it is open … but i know i have her for a more in depth search … because she is going down i have to make an inventory search of the car and can open the glove compartment and open the trunk … you see what this adds up to … the traffic stop … the charges for jail traffic … the search of the car and then i get a female officer out there to search her and behold packet of cocaine is in her jeans pocket … so from a traffic stop of failing to signal a turn i have a felony arrest … when i get her to jail i write up all the traffic offenses except for one … and for that one i write a ticket and put it in her property folder …

… why do that …

… because she will not pay it and will have a warrant on her in about three weeks and we can pull her over for an outstanding warrant … see the routine …

… sounds to me that you arrest the same people over and over …

… yes i did … i even knew those that had warrants out on them by sight … and the reason for contact is an outstanding warrant … as a matter of fact that is what jades an officer more than anything … the hooks out on bond … or even with no bail … there they are out holding up the people …

… is it true that domestic violence is the most dangerous of calls an officer can get …

… yes and no … those calls can go bad fast but we had a plan my partner and i … when we got to the porch we identified the loudest person … if after our talk with them and no one was physically injured we took the loudest one down … we had to arrest someone on all domestic violence calls … it was a city law … too many people complained about the police doing nothing that the council put it on the books that someone was going down … unless they had connections with the city … my sergeant did not like me arresting rich people … he even told me that … what are you going to do … i really had to arrest them just to cover myself … i let him figure out how to deal with the city biggies …

… that is what i meant about the new chief … he was really into pleasing the rich and the council members … he was really averse to us arresting the upper class for domestic violence so i would take them in on disturbing the peace … then the charges could not be dropped and they would have to go to court …

… the ending of my career with the dallas police department had to do with the arresting of three guys that beat up a pizza delivery girl … as it turned out it was a drug dealing scheme … she was using the pizza job to make drug deliveries … anyway the chief let them off and changed my report to compromise my partner and me …

… changed the report …

… yes … he was protecting drug dealers belonging to a city councilman …

… huh …

… oh … it gets better … i was told if i did not resign i would be fired … but the thing was the person who told me that did not have the authority to fire me … so to surprise him i resigned anyway … i could not trust the supervisors who could not trust the chief … the chief was so bad off he turned up at an officer shooting drunk … an undercover officer was killed and the chief shows up to the investigation in a taxi drunk …

… not long after the incident with my three arrestees another officer shot one of them in a drug raid and the chief brought murder charges against him … again the chief changed the report and threatened a subordinate chief to lie about it in a grand jury hearing … the subordinate chief was in the middle … if he lied it was committing perjury and if he told the truth he would be fired by the chief … at least that was the threat … so he had to come clean … the chief was arrested booked convicted and fired … by then the department was a mess from all the lackies and insiders he had promoted …

… thus ends the story of me on the force … it was a job in which i learned a lot about law enforcement and also about the control freaks that aspire to promotion …

… why do you say control freaks …

… there are two reasons for a cop to promote … one is more power and the other is too chicken to stay on the street …

… i was real insecure while all this was going down and my wife and daughter were scared of it all as they had felt intimidated by it all

… i got through the stress but it took me a long time … i can pinpoint this as the beginning of my decline …

… what did you do … without a job again …

… i was not quite there yet but after awhile i would not panic because i did not have a job … i was more insecure when i was working … anyway i had thousands of dollars saved up in vacation and comp time when i left … i decided to look elsewhere for a future … i have a thing for dallas and will not go back there … if i am on the road i will not even stop there for a rest break or gas … dallas was bad juju for me and it still sits in the back of my mind as to how much stress i was tortured by in that burg … besides it is a goat roper town anyway …

… goat roper …

… yeah … that is what we called the locals while in flight school at fort wolters …

… i went to visit my uncle in pennsylvania and get my head cleared … i knew we would not stay in dallas … i even had a few neighbors get up in my face over the incident … they believed the newspapers and the chief … hey the chief went down and i went to pennsylvania …

… it was fun to deal with my uncle … he was a wise guy …

… whoa … like in mobbed up wise guy …

… one in the same … he did not whack people … nothing like that … what he did was a little book making and a little loan sharking and some art deals …

… art deals …

… yeah …

... the art dealer ...

... it took me awhile to calm down and get back to earth ... it was hard to explain to my uncle and his girlfriend what happened ... so after awhile i tried to just let it go ... but the matter kept rattling around in my head ... i had always had problems with that ... something stressful sticking with me ... it seemed as if i did not have something to chew on in my mind i would make it up ... i knew i was hirable in the law enforcement business as i now had a degree ...

... anyway ... my uncle got shot down in a bomber over france in forty four and after that decided to live by his rules ... he figured he was living on borrowed time ... he never paid taxes ... never had a social security number ... i do not know what kind of drivers license he had as i never asked ... before you ask ... everything was in the girlfriends names ... and he went from girlfriend to girlfriend ... i only know of one that ripped him off and that was in vegas ... he was into some kind of mining interest out there ... i visited him when i was going to u s c in seventy one ...

... so it was now eighty nine and i was looking for something to do ... i was not a high roller type ... i was just looking for a living as i had a wife and daughter to support ... they were both working and i had plenty of time to find something ...

... my aunt ... my uncles sister ... had a situation with her husband who was very bad off ... he was incompetent as his mind was going ... she was much older than my uncle and needed help ... so i thought what the hey ... so i am off to new hampshire to meet with a bunch of cousins i never saw before ...

... i got in my fierro and cruised to new england ... it was good to be back on the east coast and be among a bunch of dagos i was related to ... i had never met my cousins as my father was estranged from me ... it was a real kick ...

... and instead of hunting for a job at all sorts of venues i decided to go to the department of employment security and see what they had ... something i never thought of was recommended to me ... when i left dallas the guy that told me to resign also told me i would never get a job in law enforcement again ...

... well by the time i had sold my home and moved my wife up to new hampshire ... my daughter stayed in dallas ... well soon after we got settled in concord the phone rang and i got a call from the new hampshire department of corrections ... i was going to work in a prison ... looking back on it ... well it was probably a good move at the time but i got right back into the control freak business ...

... my insecurities cropped up again and i was thinking of nothing but gloom and doom ... i jumped at the chance ... i knew my degree would be an advantage ... so off i went to the academy in the middle of a new hampshire winter but i had to stand up for myself to get there ... when i was hired i started right away without the academy ... we could work for six months without being an academy graduate ... the rule was made with the state and the union because they were so short officers ... i was a uniformed corrections officer and please do not use the word guard ... that conjures the overweight redneck prison bully ... anyway ... i learned the procedures and adapted to a whole new environment ... this was cop work without the gun ... a lot of cops i knew would never have gone into that place ... i was not intimidated by being around criminals ...

... so i was working in the prison and my wife was working for the department of transportation in a real good job dealing with the budget and payroll ... she was a good banker and always got a good job in the money and financing field ... we were doing all right ...

... i was given an assignment in the property office and learned about what the inmates could and could not have which was of benefit for cell searches ... i was on the evening shift ... and i was going on five months and had to get to the academy … then the director of security … this woman with a real control problem had the idea that i and another officer were too involved in prison functions that we could not be spared … remember we were real short of officers … so she decided that i would not be attending the academy … my question was … what about the six months rule … her idea was to allow our six months run and relieve us from employment and then rehire us … there was nothing we could do … she did not talk to us directly as that was beneath her … well to shorten the story the union got involved and went to the director about it … i was in the academy the next week … but she was a grudge holder and blamed me for the director of corrections for getting on her case … great … a control freak with a grudge …

… well the academy was a piece of cake and i graduated number one in the class … i went back on the evening shift … i was a night person and liked that shift … my second choice was the deep nights shift but it was filled by very smart people …

… why do you say that …

… no bosses around … it was a small tightly knit group …

… as things would have it with the turn over a few openings in the counselor office came open and with my degree i was in good to get one of the positions … the counselor makes mental health referrals … classification decisions …

… classification …

… yes we determine the security level of the inmate … i was assigned to work in the close custody unit … it was at level four … one level below maximum or hard lockdown … most of the inmates could not conduct themselves appropriately to be in general population … they acted up all the time and were revolving between close custody and max …

… inmates are very manipulative and try to game the system … i also ran programs for the inmates … the programs were drug and alcohol recovery training and the prison pedophile program …

… whoa … i have got to ask … what is a pedophile program …

... i thought you would ask about that ... it was called family training ...

... good grief ...

... yeah ... good grief ... the purpose of it was to get the inmate to admit their crime ... only after that would they be recommended for counseling with our metal health department ... they were still locked up but they were in a friendlier environment ...

... did any of this do any good ...

... when i first started out i was going great guns ... i really thought i was helping and was very pleased with the way things were going ... but soon i came to realize that it was all a numbers game to make the staff appear to be doing something ... in the year that i ran the family training program i had one inmate admit to his crime ... and the drug classes were for the entertainment of the inmates ... simply stated it just gave them something to do ... i became very jaded in no time ... i went from an understanding counselor to someone who knew it was all a game ... but the administration liked me as i was upping their stats ...

... getting back to the control freak ...

... maybe i was being a little hard but remember this is written with my mindset at the time ... the mania ... the depression and the insecurities ... i want those that are bipolar or have bipolar loved ones to understand how these feelings can be a normal state of mind for the bipolar ...

... that is the hardest i have seen you on anyone in the book so far ...

... oh ... it gets better than that as we go along ... a good case in point is my classifying an inmate for supermax custody ... we did not have a supermax facility ... we had level one the halfway houses ... level two were cottages outside the prison walls ... level three was general population ... level four was close custody and level five was max custody ... level six was supermax and we had to move him from our facility to colorado or illinois or california ... also we had to prove he was that much of a threat to other inmates and the staff ... well he was shipped to our max and the classification was blown off by the director of security … he killed two inmates in one day … in maximum custody … the procedures were a little lax to say the least …

… our maximum custody had the opposite of the stockholm syndrome … the officers took on the personalities of the inmates … the security staff were very difficult to work with as they were hostile and protective of the inmates … most of the officers that gravitated to duty at the maximum facility were violent to begin with and most were rageaholics and alcoholics … they treated the rest of the staff with hostility … the same way the director of security treated the staff … she would fire people left and right but she had no authority to do so …

… huh …

… yeah … she fired me once … so i went up to the personnel office and told them i was fired … i was in the deputy directors office in no time at all … he was quick to tell me i was not fired … he did not want the union and the employment commission on his case …

… so what about the crook that killed the two inmates …

… i was gone from the department by then and ended up being deposed on the case … the lawyers handling the lawsuit for the families of the dead inmates came to florida to talk to me … it seems the classification of the inmate was missing from the file … i told them that they may find the paperwork in a file in my former office … sure enough there it was … the director of security was fired and several supervisors were demoted … it was a repeat of dallas … i was two for two …

... israeli volunteer ...

... so you left the department ... when ...

... i had been there since eighty nine and left in ninety one ... i left to go to the gulf war in israel ... *what ... the gulf war ...*

... yes ... let me give you a little background ... when i was at fort bragg on my flying tour i met an israeli officer ... he was going through special forces training ... we had him over to the house ... sort of sponsored him ... he was an entebbe rescue raider ... the raid by the israelis to retrieve one hundred five kidnapped jews in uganda ...

... the fourth of july nineteen seventy six ...

... very good ...

... kind of a hard date to forget ...

... i was really into israel then and when the war broke out i had the urge to go and do my part ... it was a big time grandstand thing to do ... i quit the job at the prison and flew to tel aviv ... i went to the volunteer office ... volunteers were assigned to the sar el regiment ... the volunteers for israel regiment ... they could not assign me that day and told me to come back the next morning ... but that evening was a kicker ... there was a correspondent in the hotel where i was staying and he needed help getting his equipment up to the hilton hotel which was the headquarters for all the reporters covering the war ... when we got there with the equipment we were given press passes and a gas mask ... everybody in israel had a gas mask ... we had to take it with us at all times ... i got to sit in on press conferences and even had a scud attack that evening ... i was up half the night in the excitement not knowing what the israelis would do about the scud missles being shot into the country from iraq … the missiles caused little harm and killed no one … half the time they just hit out in the desert … anyway … it was a fun experience for me … i met another volunteer that was a british lord … he was a young man dressed in gothic attire and had safety pins in his ears … but a cool guy … it was the three of us with the press … i kept my press pass as i thought maybe i would get to tel aviv again … i had no idea where i was going … i was ready to go anywhere …

… the next morning i went to the volunteer office and was told to wait … i just hung out with the other volunteers … there were no americans there that day … and they decided to put me with the italian volunteers as i did speak a little italian … the main topic around the headquarters was not our assignments but when the israelis would get into the war … the united states must have promised the israelis the world for them not to retaliate for the scud attacks which were happening every night …

… that evening i was told i would be going to kfar hess … it was a moshaf … a commercial farm between tel aviv and jerusalem … unlike a kibbutz which was a communal operation … i use communal not communist … but the kibbutzim were formed on the same idea … i was to work on the moshaf and be ready to be called up in the event of israel getting into the war … they were surprised to meet a jew that knew how to farm … i understood the business and could operate a tractor …

… i did get to go to some training and briefings … i was never armed and never put on a uniform … i was awakened to the israeli plight … i even got to meet palestinians as the farm workers were from the west bank … the family i stayed with were super people and i got to know them real well …

… i got to go to a kibbutz for about two weeks … i can say that if i ever lived in israel i would not go to a kibbutz … i did not care for it but i met a lot of wonderful folks … the kibbutz i visited for two weeks had a lot of russian immigrants and it was fun to get to know them … i kept up the record of having never met a russian i did not like … some of them spoke very good english and many also spoke hebrew ... i went to hebrew school for half the day and then worked in the dining room ... except for the housing everything else was communal ... everyone ate in the kitchen ... the children were housed in separate quarters away from their parents ... i found that to be very strange ... not to have your children in the home ... kibbutzim are very expensive in israel ... none are self sufficient ... the kibbutz i stayed at was a few miles south of the golan heights ... there were wrecked and rusty armored vehicles out in the desert surrounding the kibbutz from the seventy three war ...

... after two weeks at the kibbutz i went back to the farm and soon departed for the united states and an uncertain future ...

... toward the edge ...

... i did not dwell on the israeli trip too much as in retrospect it was an outlandish thing to do and i did it under the guise of helping israel ... it was a absurd time in my life ...

... an absurd time ... kind of a strange way to put it ...

... i thought i was going over there to do my duty for israel and for my friend from fort bragg who was killed in the lebanon in eighty two ... but it was absolutely insane ... i quit a really good job to play mercenary ... that was essentially what i did ... i had all sorts of theme music in my head for that one ... i was going into a very deep funk ...

... a deep funk ... is that a medical term ...

... i do not know what to call it ... i believe i was in a mixed state ... both manic and depressed ... i would think up all sorts of adventures in my head and then just sit around and stare at nothing ...

... i was waiting for a summer job with the department of transportation to at least make some money ... we decided to go to florida and we bought a home there ... it was a new double wide ... we were going to retire there ... i use retirement lightly ... as i knew i had to keep working ... during my time with the department of corrections i had applied to a state department contractor to go overseas ... i would be going alone but in one year we could pay off the house ... i seemed to me to be a good trade off ... but that was just the reason i used ... i was really hunting for another adventure ...

... i worked on a road crew with the trans department ... i was part of a crew that striped the roads ... it was for the summer and we planned to leave in september of ninety one ...i actually got paid more for being on the crew than i did working at the prison in a job requiring a degree ... go figure ...

... the work was good for me ... it was physical and outside ... but i was starting to rage internally ... and i had a few outbursts on the road ... even though i was making a living i felt like a nothing ... i used to be an army officer and now i was on a road painting crew ... i felt that i was disappointing my wife and daughter ... i was disappointing myself i can tell you that ...

... you could not tell you were into the funk as you say ... did you want to do anything about it ... get help ...

... what could i do about it ... i did not know my head was screwed up ... i thought that if everybody around me just shaped up i would be all right ...

... sounds like an addict ... the resentments and all ...

... oh by then i had stopped drinking ... i did not drink for about a year maybe a year and a half before i went off the deep end ... i guess it was like an addict ... keep in mind i had been taught to blame others all my life as i knew it was them making me what i was ... my family ... as the psyches say ... my family of origin were a terrible example for me ... i was conditioned to the resentment and the rage ... it was effecting my marriage ...

... i guess so ... could you not tell that without a diagnoses ... it seems as though a lot was tearing at you all at once ...

... all i can say is that i was getting worse ... but worse at what i did not know ... one of the things about the military was the change in environments and in my civilian life i tried to repeat it ...

... a geographical cure as they call it ...

... no not that ... i was in no need to get fixed as i thought there was nothing wrong with me ... i was not looking for a mental fix ... at least i did not look at it that way at the time ... i just lived with myself the way i was which was not a very happy existence ... looking back i may not have been able to cope in the prison ... i lost any empathy for the inmates and was just going through the motions as a counselor ... so the road work came at the right time ... i worked through september and then on to florida ...

… we had been to florida before and we were to live only a few blocks from my wifes sister and her husband … we got along great with them …

… i had no idea what i was going to do … we had put enough away so that neither of us had to work for awhile … i really liked the home and it only cost twenty one thousand … today that home would sell for over a hundred grand …

… we got settled in and i started looking around … i thought of maybe getting on a road crew and then promoting up … but the starting salary was around seventeen thousand a year …

… only seventeen a year … how can anyone make a living on that …

… it was florida … it was typical of the wages in the state … i have no idea how it is now but i suspect it is not much better …

… i take it your were not about to work for that …

… it was one thing to be on a road crew but for eight bucks an hour … in the sun … at least i had enough sense not to pursue that … then i noticed an ad in the paper about being an investment banker … as it turned out that is just a fancy name for a stock broker … i called for an interview … it was the best move i could have made … it was the smartest step i had taken since retirement … pre meltdown that is …

… how so …

… we had never saved much and did not know how to make money … we had my retirement which kept the wolves at bay through all my joblessness … we could have lived off the retirement in our new home but it would have been a sorry state … i was not looking to make a fortune so i could take a commissioned only job …

… i was set up for an initial interview … now let me tell you this … i know how to interview … i know how to present myself in a positive light … and the interview went well … the h r guy did not promise me the world but i took him to mean i could make a lot of money … how i would do it i did not know but i was willing to give it a try … he set me up for several tests to determine my suitability for the training … it was an all day affair … they were aptitude tests … it was an easy task … i was under no stress to pass as i had not invested anything in the job … it was odd … i normally would be all keyed up for something like that … but the retirement pay gave me a sense of security as our living expenses were very low …

… during our stay in new hampshire we were able to pay off our bills … so into the tests i went … i thought it would be a real brain drain … it was about the level of a tenth grade battery of aptitude tests … when i finished i knew i would be accepted … and i was …

… next came the training for the license … after the first day i was convinced i would not make it and all of those old feeling would come back … and they did … i felt as though my reputation was a stake … how could i face the world if i did not pass the test … my ego was so out of control i thought everyone was watching me struggle with the classes … there were about twenty in the class … and what i found strange was there were no women …

… i had heard that that stock brokering is a mens game …

… the course lasted for six weeks and then you were on your own with the study guide … i had acquired several different additions of the study guide from a half priced used bookstore … when i felt i was ready i was to call them … the company staff that is … i was to call them and they would make an appointment for me to take the test … i was in tampa and the test was in orlando so i would have to stay overnight before the test …

… i studied on the local campus cafeteria instead at home … it did me good to get out of the house … i answered four hundred questions a day five days a week for six weeks … i burned through the math so that i had the formulas for options and commissions and taxes and anything else with a number … in a month and a half i felt i was ready for the test … off i went to orlando … well i was not ready for the test … i failed it by one question … and to add to my problems on the way back the carburetor went out on the car … it was a really bad day … i called the brokerage firm and told them … no i actually went in and handed my books over to them … why i did that i do not know but i just handed them the books and walked away …

… i was disgusted with myself … but in a few days they called and told me to come in … they set me up for another round of classes …

i put my tail between my legs and went in to pick up my books ... the h r people were real kind and seemed to think it was no big thing ...

... in a week i started the course all over again ... about two thirds of the class were my former class members and the instruction staff was not the same as before ... something had gone wrong that so many of us had botched the test ... when we got to options ... which was about a fifth of the test we were taught an entire different set of formulas ... it had to be the options ... i was still not very confident ... i had a hard time getting over the failure ... i do not like failing anything ... especially when my livelihood depended on it ...

... i had learned a lot about the finance business and had a lot of questions about the company ... it seems they paid forty percent of the commission back to the broker ... so i ran the numbers in my head ... with a million in sales the company would get five percent or fifty thousand and they in turn pay us forty percent of that which amounts to twenty thousand dollars ... i would have to sell three million in stocks bonds and mutual funds to make sixty grand a year ... i would have to pull in some big fish to do that ...

... i was naïve about how i would get the accounts ... i was thinking way ahead of myself ... i had to pass the test first ... again back to four hundred questions a day for six weeks but with better formulas and more confidence ... the second time around i passed it no sweat and was on my way to the trading floor ...

... i was told i would have to get my own leads ... i would have to decide who to call and what to present to them ... and i would make not a dime while trying to figure this all out ... no money at least until i sold something ... or as it is put ... until i bought a security for someone ...

... then the phone rang ... i had been accepted by the state department contractor ... it had been a year since my application ... i felt desperate for some money and jumped at the chance ... i would almost die ...

… bolivia and back to the money …

… what a suck hole bolivia is …

… you seem to be getting an edge on you … bolivia is a suck hole … what is up …

… i am doing my best to give you the me of then … my life was unraveling and i did not see it … first israel and now bolivia …

… under the guise of paying off the house …

… guise is right … i just craved adventure and could not get enough of it …

… why do you think that was … looking back on it now …

… for one thing i was so miserable at home because i was causing so much of a problem for my wife and my daughter … even though my daughter did not live with us she was worried … it was as if i could not think two thoughts on the same subject … so off i go to washington for training with the state department and then about a two month wait and on to bolivia … i was originally to go to moscow … but that fell through …

… a guy got sick in bolivia and came back so i volunteered to go … i should have checked into it more … gotten some background material … a lot of the people assigned to bolivia were med evaced back to the states …

… what kind of training did you do …

… anything from police work to paperwork and when i got there all we did was paperwork … i was a cheap clerk for the state department … it sounds like an adventure but in reality is was a desk job …

… i did however have a lot of contact with the locals and was doing very well in my spanish although i could not conjugate verbs

167

worth a darn … so i got a lot of strange looks when i tried to speak in the past tense …

… so why do you call it a suck hole …

… i was able to live very well but the locals … the indian population … were very poor … the infrastructure was very limited … parts of the city … the slums where the indian population lived did not have modern facilities … they lived at the subsistence level … i on the other hand had a nice apartment … well three of us lived in the apartment and we had a maid …we treated her real well with extra food and extra money from time to time … it was a way of us not being the ugly americans …

… the population had a lot of resentment towards the americans and the europeans … you could feel it when you went into businesses … except the restaurants … we americans are very big tippers …

… i busied myself with going to spanish classes and reading … i also was writing a book about the second world war experiences of a jewish officer in the canadian army in europe … it had to do with the end of the war and israel … refugees going to israel … it was fun to write … one day i may take it out and spruce it up for submission …

… so the excitement you thought you would have was a paperwork drill …

… more or less … but you have to admit that just packing up and going to bolivia was a little off the wall …

… were you having the usual theme music playing in your head …

… oh yes … when we landed i looked around and the airport looked like something out of a mercenary movie … there were even two c forty sevens pushed off to the side of the runway … the place looked bombed out … my first thought was what have i gotten myself into …

… from the last chapter you said you almost died …

… yeah … i contracted typhoid fever … when the doctor said that i came out of my stupor and sat straight up … if i had not been in bolivia i may well have died … the staff at the hospital knew how to handle the disease …

... of course if you had not been in bolivia you would not have gotten the disease ...

... good point ... i thought of that myself ... i was in the hospital for a week and had been in for three days before anyone from the embassy came to see me ... i found out they were trying to get out of the hospital bill and were about to fire me ...

... for being in the hospital ...

... yes ... it was a totally mercenary operation and the insurance company simply did not wish to pay so they were going to lay the bill off on me ... from the third day on they kept calling to see when i would be discharged ... not one of them ... at least what i can remember ... not one of them asked me how i was doing ... i had become a problem ... now i understood why the turn over was so great in bolivia ...

... i was out of the hospital about a week and had a relapse ... not the fever coming back but just illness that had me weakened ... i am sure the altitude had something to do with it ...

... altitude ...

... yes ... la paz is twelve thousand feet up ... to give you an idea what that is like for someone my size ... six two and two twenty ... well it takes a lot of pumping for my heart to keep me going ... when i was in d c i was training for the moscow marathon ... i was up to sixteen miles about three times a week ... when i got to bolivia i went out to run ... i made it about a mile and a half and had to sit down on the curb before i feel down ... it was a very tough environment ...

... how did you get typhoid fever ...

... something i ate or drank ... i only ate at the restaurants on the good side of town ... i just got something that was tainted ... on top of the typhoid fever i had salmonella ...

... good grief ...

... typhoid and salmonella are a good combination if you wish to lose weight ... i lost about twenty five pounds in a couple of weeks ... anyway ... i was still sick after about three weeks ... i threw in the towel and told them i was leaving ... it was nothing they could do

… they wanted an open ended contract with us which made it open ended on both sides … so i bought a ticket and went back to florida …

… how long did it take you to get over your illness …

… it was like a seasick person stepping off the boat and onto the dock … when i hit the two hundred feet altitude in florida it was only a few days until i was okay … i was all right physically but it the head … well that was another matter …

… explain please …

… i was down … depressed over another job failure … i was going through jobs now … in less than two years i had been in four jobs … as i went back to the broker business …

… but you said you did not make any money before …

… oh i had a few accounts when i started out … my wife was working there now and the firm changed their policy and were paying an hourly rate against commission … it was a low wage but it took the pressure off … between my wife and me … well with the retirement we were doing real well … i thought i had a new attitude toward the work and really dug in … at this point i was glad to be alive …

… alive …

… yeah that was about the only thing i had to be grateful for …

… seems like a slim margin to have as an attitude toward your life …

… i did not think of making a living nor did i think of my wife … all i could think of was getting up for work everyday and being distracted … no that is the wrong word … all i could think of was the numbers running around in my head …

… numbers …

… a broker lives with that every day … the markets the stocks the bonds the mutual funds … i was very good at getting leads … when i got back to the firm … and i was thankful they took me back … i was put in a training program that the firm just started … we were not thrown out on the floor and forced to do or die as far as commissions went … the firm wised up as they were going through people like crazy … actually the greedy management was just training and licensing people for other firms … but now they concentrated on keeping people … the training concentrated on getting leads and presentation … i cut my presentation from about a page and a half of banter to a few words …

… did the company let you do that … do they not have scripts. …

… as i said at the start of the book all i said was my name is jon langione i am a stockbroker … may i send you my card … but it is what i learned about the system and how one can make money without spending a lot of time to do it …

… now you really have my attention …

… ask yourself this … why pay commissions … why pay someone to do something that you can do yourself …

… i think we all do that because the broker is the expert …

… expert schexpert … no … you do that because you are afraid to make choices with your money … you lay it off on someone else … i do not mean to get too tough with you but think about it … if you call a broker and ask if it the right time to buy stock is the broker going to say no … and why pay five percent for a mutual fund if you can get one at no commission called a no load fund …

… are not the commissioned funds better funds … managed better …

… no they just cost you five percent …

… but would i not have to keep up with the accounts everyday …

… i do … it takes me about five minutes … and when you combine all your accounts at one discount firm it is like controlling a little hedge fund … just think of having the sal luca big money fund …

… sounds kind of cool … but i have to tell you i know very little about investing …

… i will give you a few books that will get you on your way … the books and an account with a discount firm is all you need … but i am getting way ahead …

… it was at the peak of me starting to get a handle on the broker business that i realized two things … one was that i was up to my neck in myself and could not get out of it … and two … i was taking advantage of folks that did not know the investing system which did not set well with my self esteem … whatever that is … i had hit the wall and was on a flight to the west coast … if this chapter seems a little jumbled it is because i was jumbled and everything came together in my head … i would have numbers going around in my noggin all day long and then come home and watch the business channels … the numbers were a diversion from myself … i had to think about something else to stay away from the horrible feeling about what i had become … it was the decision maker …

… what was the decision maker …

… it was when i could no longer cope with what i had become … i did not know what it was but i had that moment of clarity … that one moment when i knew i had to do something and get professional help … so i called the one eight hundred number …

… do you see how backwards i am relating this to you … putting the cart before … well you get my meaning …

… yes i can see it …

… it was the way i was …

… you could not think straight …

… i thought i was but then realized i was not …

… the moment of clarity … like an addict almost …

… i was an addict … i was addicted to my own process of thinking … my brain fed off of my system … i was pulled down physically … my brain pulled me down more than the typhoid fever …

… i was near collapsing and could do nothing but lie there and stare into the darkness … except for the tiny bit of energy i had left to get on to the plane … but i could not help but think i was on a new adventure and even had the old theme music churning in my head … but i was still tied to the broker business … i bought two financial papers to read on the way to the west coast … the flight is a blur … somehow it felt like a few minutes instead of five hours … i landed in los angeles and was met by a limo driver hired by the hospital … i got my bags and stepped out into the night … it was cold and raining …

… yeah … it was a dark and stormy night …

... clinic of the gaga ...

... now we are getting to the recovery as it is called ...

... never understood what that word meant ... recovery ... sounds like upholstering does it not ... it is part of the catch phrases the mentally ill or addicts ... addicts think they are mentally ill ... it is a way of laying off their behavior ... we will get into that as we go along ...

... so it was raining and cold when you arrived ...

... yes it was march of ninety three .

... did you feel that you were finally going to get some help ... finally facing the monster ...

... good way to put it ... i do not know what my expectations were ... i was in a daze ... i was in a state of confusion ... i had a moment of clarity ... but it was only a moment ... it did not last through the trip ... i knew i had called the clinic and that i was ticketed to go to los angeles ... but by the time i got there i did not know what for ...

... really ...

... true as i can be ... i had no idea why i assigned myself to the world of mental health care ... i just knew it was an act of desperation ...

... so you went from desperation to clarity to desperation ...

... that about sums it up ... i went into the darkness so to say ... and it was exciting ... going to los aangeles was one of the most exciting ventures i ever took ... i was thrilled to be there ... if you can believe it i was elated and depressed at the same time ... i was in a mixed state of mania and depression ... one hope i had was that if i knew what was wrong i could then fix it ...

... on your own with no meds ...

... being put on meds did not cross my mind that night ...i just wanted to get started on whatever journey it would take me ...

... what did you arrive to ...

... i do not understand ...

... i guess i could have put that a better way ... tell me about your arrival ... tell me about the reception you received ...

... the limo pulled into the parking lot of a small square building ... there was a building behind it with three separate wings ... the parking lot was well lit ... i expected to walk into a situation that i may not have been able to escape from ...

... you thought you were going to be locked in ...

... yes i did ... i did not know what to expect ... it was all guesswork for me ... the driver carried my bag into the lobby ... there was no one there to meet me ... the driver told me to have a seat and he walked to the rear of the clinic ... in a minute or two an orderly came out and introduced himself ... he picked up my bag and told me to follow him ... we walked down a hallway to a nurses station ... again i was told to take a seat ... the nurse ... she had a nametag with r n on it ... the nurse asked me why i was here ... i told her t m u ... totally messed up ... she said she understood and that if i knew why i was there i would probably not be there ... that statement confused me even more ... the orderly showed me to my room and then asked me to open my suitcase ... he riffled through my clothes and toiletries for ... i guess drugs or weapons ... he asked me if i was on any drugs or had i used drugs in the past ...

... i told him i had never used any drugs ... which was the truth ... in my life i have never even smoked marijuana much less mainlined coke or heroin ... the last thing i needed was drugs is what i told him ... his remark was that i was here for recovery ... my reply was recovery from what ... i had never heard the word used in that context before ... he told me to go back to the nurses station and have a seat ...

… the nurse asked me a laundry list of questions … again about drugs and if i was on any sort of medication … not just for my mental health but any kind of medication …

… i got to thinking about the questions from the orderly and the nurse … what i was doing is called self reporting … another mental health piece of jargon … but they took in what i told them and filled out a form … the nurse told me that i had a nine a m appointment with the doctor and that breakfast starts at seven … she told me an orderly will come get me the first morning to show me around … she offered me a sedative … i think i refused as in the past i had no trouble sleeping … or at least told her that … i cannot really remember if i took something or not … i was not inclined to take prescriptions … anyway i went to bed … it was about one in the morning and i had some jet lag so i went right off to sleep …

… i never really thought of it … the self reporting … if there are no outside referrals there is nothing to go on but what the patient tells the doctor or nurse …

… yes … some mental health professionals use only self reporting … which to me is an easy way of getting over or getting what you want … especially addicts and alcoholics …

… i got up before the orderly came in and got myself squared away for the day … i was going to impress the doctor with my stability … no really … that is the way i felt … i was more manic in the morning … breakfast and then back to the room to await the doctors appointment … what i did not realize for the longest time is that when i spoke i spoke very rapidly … to me it was my normal speech pattern … i did not know that other people found it a little overwhelming … i would also bounce from topic to topic in the middle of a sentence …

… did not your wife say anything about this … the speech pattern …

… by the time i ended up in the clinic my wife was worn down … me going to the clinic was as much as a break for her as it was for me … this was a lot different than the trips to israel or bolivia … this was very serious … i just did not take it that way in the beginning … i took it as a test for me …

... like the brokers exam ...

... essentially ... i had no idea what i would have to do to pass ... but i was up for it that morning ... bring it on ... the doctor would be impressed by me . i was out of my depression on a quick turn to mania ... that is how fast i cycled ... i was that way in the brokerage firm ... one call would put me in a slump and another would raise me up ...

... the doctor was a mild mannered sort ... i guessed he had seen it all ... i sat and rambled on about who knows what ... within about twenty minutes after some general questions he told me i was bipolar ... now i had not heard much about the disorder ... except what i had seen on t v and in the movies ... the medication he gave me was typical for bipolar ... he told me it would be a few weeks before i saw the effect ... i asked him how long i would be staying ... he reply was about a month ...i asked him if there was any way i could work through the illness without medication ... he lowered the boom when he told me that the salt compound he was giving me might not work and if not we would move on to something else ... but even in my fog i understood that i would be prescribed some sort of meds and would have to take them for the rest of my life ... back into a blue funk ... he also ordered a blood test for me ... i guessed the test was for checking the veracity of my self reporting ...

... so you were just left to hang around for several weeks ...

... not at all ... after breakfast i noticed the other patients walking to one of the wings on the building out back ... it appeared they were going to some kind of meeting ... i never heard of a group session until then ... again i saw them in the movies ... but to tell you the truth i never understood what they were for ...

... i went to my room and jumped onto the bed ... i was in the room alone ... i had nodded to a few folks in the rec room where breakfast was served ... but i had no one to ask about the meetings ... i feel asleep ...

... i was awakened by an orderly to go to lunch ... again i stayed to myself ... i normally jumped right into the middle of things ... but after my meeting with the doctor i did not want the people in the clinic to know what was wrong with me ...

... back to the wrong with you bit ... seems you have gone full circle ...

... well i was naïve as to mental illnesses ... here i had been an army officer and now i was a mental cripple ... that is the way i felt about it ... i was defective ... i could not wait for the meds to kick in ... i had to go to the nurses station three times a day for my script ... i will only mention medication or scripts or doses ... it will not talk about a particular med by name ... it may give other folks with bipolar the idea it would work for them and may lead them to self medicate ...

... good idea ... back to your not wanting anyone to know you were bipolar ... why ... you were in a clinical situation ... you were there because you were sick and wanted to get well ...

... well ... this is a little hard to explain ... i thought i was well ... i did not believe i had mental health problems ...

... but you were in a psyche clinic ...

... it was the illness ... i needed help but i was all right ...

... that does not compute ...

... why should it compute ... i was in the throes of mental illness ... i was bipolar ... i had not made sense for quite some time ...

... but you had all those responsible jobs ... you must have made sense to someone ...

... like all those with bipolar ... we find out that acting comes easy ... i would get the jobs and then immediately feel insecure about it ... i had not held any of the jobs for more than two and a half years ... and these were good jobs with all sorts of benefits and pensions attached ... i felt it was normal to just quit and run ... and by the time i retired i had quit and run from about everything ... going to the clinic was a cut and run ... it was my normal behavior but it was not normal behavior if you catch my drift ...

... being a very impatient person i wanted to get on with this cure ... i wanted to get this bipolar thing under control ... i had to do something ... so after lunch on the first day i went to the nurses station to take my second pill and i asked where everybody was going ... she told me they were going to group ... i asked how i could get into a group just for something to do ...

    ... the nurse understood that i felt i would just languish for a couple of weeks ... she made a phone call and then had an orderly take me to a room with about fifteen people in it ... there was a young lady who was in charge ... she asked me my name telling me we use only first names ... when i said jon everyone in the group said welcome jon ... she then asked me if i would share with the room why i was there ... i sucked it up and told everyone i was there because i was bipolar ... with that she went back to a man who was sharing when i came in ... sharing that is another piece of mental health jargon ...

    ... you seem to find fault with the jargon ...

    ... actually i am getting ahead of myself ... more will be revealed ...

    ... ah so ...

    ... i was still in a blue funk and had a little jet lag left over ... but i was lucid enough to listen and take in the sharing ... i remember one guy from that first group ... it was a new englander with long blond hair who could do nothing all day except sit around and smoke dope which his working wife paid for ... though she did not speak there was a woman of about thirty covered in tattoos ... after a few of the group spoke i came to realize that this was an addicts group ... after the meeting i asked the monitor if there was a group for those with bipolar disorder ... she told me that as far as she knew i was the only one in the clinic that was bipolar ... then she asked me what was my drug of choice ... not knowing exactly what she meant i told her i was prescribed the medication the doctor put me on this morning ... no she said what illegal drugs have i been taking ... it seemed to me she had a limited range of experience in the mental health field ... even as a new member of the american bipolar league i could figure that out ...

    ... the meeting lasted about two hours and i was told another group was forming for the next session in the room and i was welcome to stay ... the second meeting was a repeat of the first except with a different moderator ... again i tried to stay in the shadows and was not bothered to share anything … half of the group in the last session returned for this one …

… i came to believe that this was to be the tenor of the meetings … i felt bad that i was not addicted to anything … i would soon present myself as addicted just to fit in …

… what …

… yes … i did not say i was addicted to anything in particular but that i was addicted to my behavior … it took me about two weeks to get around to that … meantime i went to all the twelve step meetings i could and generally just listened to the stories … i heard some real horror tales from people that i thought it was amazing that they were still alive …

… i had good stories stored in my head but i was sure no one wanted to hear jump or flying stories … or about my days on the street as a cop … or my adventures working in the prison … half of the patients were sponsored by the state and remanded into the clinic as a provision of their probation …i could see the difference in the motivation of the patients … there was a difference between the parolees and the self admitted … i do not know if there were any patients committed to the clinic as i never went over to the other wings of the building …

… i was not allowed to go to outside programs for about a week and had to be there two weeks before i could take a saturday trip … the clinic had outings … but like any other day they had groups … they had groups galore …

… what … just monitors that were in the clinic dealing with twelve step programs …

… essentially … depending upon the facilitator some of the meeting were a little tougher …

… tougher … how so …

… we were required to bring out the real gut feeling not just the surface stuff … in my case i had a lot of surface stuff … lack of understanding as to how people treated me and my own thought processes getting in my way … until i made myself an alcoholic i did not fit in very well with the groups …

... hold on ... until you made yourself an alcoholic ...

... yes ... i did it to fit in ... to belong to something ...

... you never talked about a drinking problem ...

... i did not have a drinking problem ... i was a wine and brandy sipper ... in retrospect i self medicated ... but as far as being addicted to it ... well i was not ... i never had a d w i ... never laid in my own filth like the horror stories i heard ... i just needed to belong to something ... but first let me tell you about my first twelve step meeting outside the clinic ... i went across the street to a church basement to a codependents anonymous meeting ... by now i had the system down as far as the conduct expected in the meeting ... what i was developing though was staying in my head all the time ...

... explain ...

... follow along ... the codependents meeting was fun ... i never heard some of the things i did in there ...

... can you talk about it ... i know the meetings are secret in context ...

... secret only that you do not rat out the sharers name ... but i have some great stories from twelve step programs ...

... i thought what was discussed in the meeting was privileged ...

... you mean like clergy contritent or doctor patient ...

... yes ...

... well no ... there is no right of confidentiality ... if you say you robbed the local convenience store with a gun while drunk ... everyone in the room can be used as a witness against you ... this has happened in cases where the twelve stepper admitted to a murder ... nope no rights against incrimination ...

... i am sorry we got off the track a bit ...

... no sweat ... now back to the codependents anonymous meeting ... it was a hoot ... the people in it were doing the same things over and over expecting different results ... this one guy married three illegal alien mexican women and their families showed up for him to support ... a woman in the group kept dating convicts ...

... how can you date a convict ...

… go visit him … but she kept talking about this great boyfriend she had … and in each case all they were doing was getting her to put money into their canteen account … you know … to buy candy and soda … but she kept doing it …

… then it dawned on me that i had been doing the same thing by changing locations and changing jobs … with each location change i would think i was on the right track and with a job change i would think i now have a new career established … in effect i was doing the same thing over and over expecting different results …

… that is the definition of insanity is it not …

… in psycho jargon babble it is but in reality it is a common state of the human psyche … it is not insanity but it defines the cycles we get into that cause our life to be a wreck … the more i went to these meetings and groups the more i realized how much of a wreck my life was …

… how did you define your state of mind … how were you a wreck …

… i could not hold anything together … i started to share in the groups at the clinic and mostly i blamed others for my lot in life … if everyone would just shape up i would be okay …

… now that is an addict … that is common among the resentful … were you resentful …

… oh yes …i would see other people at work getting along and doing well and all i could think of was how my life was such a struggle … but what i started to do was typical of the beginning twelve stepper … i started to measure everything i did … i was also beginning to fill up a lot … i was on the verge of crying … the medication was beginning to set in …

… after about the first week i began to go out to a a groups … i was finally in a place where i belonged …

… did you really believe that …

… yes i did … i was surrounded by what i had grown up with …

… back to your family of origin …

… yes … i understood the craziness of it all and settled in to being a member of the group … however … and this is a big however … i did not relate to the stories … i did not relate to the financial wrecks people made of themselves because of going on month long benders … or because of going on gambling binges … i also noticed that the people with only a little time away from the booze had the most answers … it was like i am all better now … sorry for all the mess i made … but one thing did ring true for me was the mess i was making of my life … but in two weeks i had not met one other bipolar patient or person … i did however meet a lot of criminals remanded into the a a program … i went to one n a meeting …

… narcotics anonymous …

… yeah … it was a coven of witches i swear … it was the most demented group of people i had ever been around … i discussed it with one of the group monitors back at the clinic … i figured he was the best one to talk to about it … before he got his p h d he used to shoot loads …

… loads …

… yes get this … he would fill the needle with codeine and cocaine and heroin and meth and shoot it into his veins all at once … i was surprised he had a brain let much less a doctorate … he also got folks to bring up the worst in themselves … to get it out so to say … but he recommended i go to no more n a meetings …

… what was the worst in you …

… i expressed how much of a loser i was … the longer i spent in the clinic the more i was convinced i was useless … the twelve step meetings were having a very adverse effect on me … i felt i could not keep up with all the people in recovery … i felt i was so bad off that i was not worth the time of a sponsor … but i ended up with one anyway … he was a retired marine fighter pilot … so we had a lot in common … he got me to the first five steps … the personal inventory stage and he told me to get caught up on my chips for months of sobriety … by then i had about twenty months … something like that … most of the meeting i went to were held in this convention hall … it may have been a union hall in the old days … hundreds of people filtered through there … they would have guest speakers … one was a rock and roller with one of the top groups in the world … cannot mention his name of course … i liked the guest speakers they were entertaining … after all it was los angeles … it was show business …

… so tell me about your personal inventory …

… i wrote it with my sponsor … it was about all the things i did in my drunkenness …

… but you were not a drunk …

… oh i just made stuff up … stuff that was conceivable … remember i had to belong to something … and like the folks at the clinic i would tell everyone how long i had been in recovery … and the meds were not doing a bit of good except to make me feel melancholy … i did not know that though … i thought that was the way i would feel as a cured bipolar … the staff did not recognize the stuff was not taking effect because i made myself appear to be better … but deep down inside i knew that once i left the clinic not very much would change and i was running out of stories to tell about myself … i could not keep up with the tales in the clinic groups …

… such as …

… well this lady … the one with the tattoos i told you about … well she was remanded into the program by the judge and was under investigation for murder … turns out she shot up her boyfriend with heroin and he overdosed and died right there next to her in the bed … when she came out of the stupor there he was dead and stiff right next to her … she waited a day to call for help which did not sit well with the authorities … one thing i did not have to contend with was the authorities … then i got a roommate …

… his whole family was in the clinic … his wife and children were in another wing … this is a juicy story …

… go on …

… well they were both schoolteachers … they had two teenage boys and for some reason he felt compelled to tell his wife of eighteen years that he put himself through college by being a boy toy for some gay guy … his wife went off the deep end and gained two hundred pounds and somehow his oldest son found out about it and lit the school on fire … after all those years of marriage he decided he was gay after all … now get this …

... this is a good one ... go no ...

... well the clinic psyches thought it would be good for him to explore his gay side so they directed him to gay bars and allowed him to prowl at night ... i found this method of cure to be very strange ... he was a good guy and a hoot to talk to ... but even in my funk i thought something is not right ... not all the counselors had their stuff together ... give you an example ... one of the group monitors came in one day and was distraught ... it seems she was a badminton referee and had a bad experience over the weekend because no one paid attention to her calls ... she broke down and started to cry ... the entire session was taken up with her badminton experience ... but by then i just wrote it off to being another bad experience in the gaga clinic ...

... but i was having fun ... i went to one meeting after the other all night and all day ... i listened to the stories and became drawn in by the drama of it all ... by the third weekend i was able to go on saturday outings ... i was diagnosed as high functional ... whatever that was ... ah ... that is another point in the twelve step meetings ... every alcoholic hits bottom before they go into recovery ... i was considered to have a high bottom and be high functional ... i was passing the test ... between the groups the outings and the good meals ... well ... i was having a good time ... also i did not want to go home ... so after my thirty day stay in the clinic i elected to go to a halfway house ... the expense for that was not covered by insurance and would have to come out of my pocket ...

... there were about twelve guys in the house and there was one i hit it off with ... we went to meetings together as i had a car ... a rental ... the halfway house counselor was a recovering cocaine addict that had a real bad attitude ... he seemed to have the answer to everyones problems ... oh and he was under indictment for dealing ... welcome to the los angeles addict scene ... the meetings we went to were in different locations then the meetings that i was taken to by the clinic ... i spent two weeks at the halfway house and decided it was time to get out of there and go home ...

… i was beginning to feel unique as i had yet to find another bipolar person … i did however develop the dumb habit of telling just about everyone i knew that i was bipolar … i got a lot of strange looks … so back to tampa … thus ended my time at the gaga clinic and i knew that i was returning in exactly the same condition as when i left … one thing never dawned on me …

… what was that …

… it was the idea that i needed to change my behavior … i still thought i was doing just fine …

… if everyone else would just shape up …

… except that now i had a bunch of meetings to go to … being unemployed … well the meetings at least got me out of the house …

... less than zero ...

... the first thing i did when i got home was tell everyone i was a bipolar alcoholic ... i had not spoken to my wife very much in the last six weeks ... i was ashamed that i had to put her through what i did ... i was right back in the same environment ... but i knew i would not go back to the brokerage firm ... she was working there and i did not to want to go through another high stress meltdown ...

... i looked for twelve step meeting ... there was a central number in the phone book so i called and got a list of a a meetings in the local area ... i wrote a location down but got the time wrong ... i went over to the meeting house ... it was used only for twelve step meetings ... i arrived and walked into the only meeting room that had people collecting in it ... it turned out to be an al anon meeting ... i had heard of it but did not go to one in los angeles ... it was a totally different environment ... it was for people who had to deal with alcoholics ... they got to the family of origin topic very quickly ... i felt i was in the right place ... the people who shared told of the difficulty of being involved with an addict ... and many spoke of their childhood ... being with addicts and alcoholics as they were growing up ...

... i was not asked to share but was welcomed ... i told them i was a bipolar alcoholic and a few asked me to explain my alcoholism ... i did not make up any stories ... i was asked to keep coming back to al anon ... and because it was a twelve step group to keep going to the a a meetings ...

... this lady said she would likc to get to know me and my background ... within a week she was my sponsor ... you normally do not have a sponsor of the opposite sex … but al anon is mostly women … plus i had a feeling she had her stuff together …

… how did your wife take to a female sponsor …

… not well but she gave me the benefit of the doubt … after awhile my sponsor told me that i can keep up with the a a meetings but she believed al anon was more important to me … i felt that if i did not go to a a meetings i would appear to be a person who fell off the wagon …

… i was still cycling the depression and mania … i had a psych at the air force base in tampa and he kept me on the same meds … and the meds were absolutely useless … but like a good soldier i kept taking them … i thought that sometime … soon i hoped … that sometime i would be overcome with the cure and the meds would miraculously bring me to a state of sanity that would be noticed by those around me and everyone would congratulate me … meanwhile with all the meetings i was spending a lot of time in my head … i also had to find a job …

… in a moment of total insanity i called the florida department of corrections and asked about employment … i was told by human resources that there were jobs galore … the woman asked me about my background and when i told her i had a b a in criminal justice she recommended i apply for a probation officer position … i asked where there were openings … when she got to key west i jumped all over it …

… what …

… sure … it sounded like a good idea to go to a tropical paradise … plus i was running again … my behavior and emotions and thinking did not change one bit … i just spent six weeks on a hospital vacation … i also sent applications to other local agencies … but the first one to answer were the key west folks … i went down and stayed overnight before the interview … now common sense should have told me not to go down there on any permanent basis …

… why is that …

… the expense of the place … i stopped by a motel to check in and it was three hundred fifty five a night … for a lousy motel … so i drove to the naval base and asked if they had guest quarters … the gate guard directed me to the officers quarters … i got a room for six bucks … another great benefit of a military retirement …

… i went to the interview and knew i had the job … i was more than qualified and they were short four officers … what they did not tell me was that key west was the pariah of the florida department of corrections … and i knew in my gut that i did not want to work for the woman in charge of the place … she had alcoholic written all over her … but i did not go with my gut and allowed them to submit my application …

… why did you not go with your gut feeling … usually that is the best course … to go with your intuition that is …

… i was into wishful thinking … i believed i could make it right … of course i told them i was an alcoholic in recovery and that i was bipolar …

… you did not …

… it was almost the first thing out of my mouth …

… did you come to regret it …

… i came to regret that i ever saw the place … but in about a month i was off to the probation officers academy … i think it was about nine weeks long and i had to live there … it was all the way across the state from tampa in lauderhill north of fort lauderdale … this was my third academy …

… i quickly came to the assumption that most of the students were over their heads and had no idea what they were getting into … a lot of them had degrees in social work and thought that what they would be doing was social work … they were going to change the criminals … kum bah ya … it was not long before i announced to the class …

… that you were an alcoholic and bipolar … what was the reason for doing that … what was your motivation …

… what was my motivation … you sound like an acting coach … let us see … my motivation … looking back on it i think i used it to excuse my behavior …

… was your behavior that bad … if i can use the word bad … i am trying to find the context …

… that is all right … i think i did it for the shock value … i would get strange looks … and i loved the drama of it all … most of the class was under twenty five and i must have appeared a true aberration … no i was an aberration … a walking wacko … that plus the fact that i was on the key west staff … i was a double pariah …

… i went back to tampa on a few of the weekends but mostly i stayed to myself and went to al anon meetings in the evening … i may have gone to an a a meeting or two but i remember there were not many around that area …

… i poured myself into the academy and did well … but i kept getting that gut feeling that i was in over my head emotionally … i was still on the same meds and i was raw most of the time … i had to work at not crying sometimes and i felt strange …

… *strange … how is that …*

… anxious … i guess you can call it that … i was anxious and agitated … i was getting blood tests about once a month to check the meds levels and the doctor kept upping the dose … so the meds were catching on but not in a therapeutic way … i was keyed up all the time and try as i may was not fitting in except with the staff going to the keys …

… *was being a key west officer that bad … i know i used bad again … what was it with the key westers …*

… one we were a very small group … if any of the supervisors wanted to visit it took a two day trip … we were a subunit of the main office and our boss was sent there to get rid of her at the main office … all this came out during the academy … i found the supervisory staff to be very much in love with themselves … again … just like the dallas police department and the new hampshire department of corrections all you heard out of the bosses mouths was how you can be fired …

… *again with the control freaks …*

… you got it …

… i went to the keys about two weeks before graduation and looked for a place … i found a small … very small efficiency apartment for over six hundred dollars plus utilities … i soon discovered that key west was extremely expensive and i also learned a lot about vacation spots and the folks that lived there …

… like what …

… because of the climate there were a lot of homeless and the place was overrun with drugs … the saying in the office was … arrive on vacation and leave on probation … and it was not a joke … i got settled into my place over the next weekend and after i finished the course i started work with a case load of nearly one hundred forty probationers …

… that sounds a little high to me …

… it was unmanageable … half of them were homeless and not to be found … the paperwork for the whole caseload was about six months behind … the first thing i had to do was to prioritize the files as to the date of end of probation … a report was due the court on everybody getting off supervision … if the report was not done in time the court could hold the probation officer in contempt … i worked straight out for about two weeks to catch up … i was very good at the paperwork part and it was noticed … in fact the whole job was paperwork and drug tests … there was a drug testing system called fast track that would indicate the drugs in the probationers urine … half of them popped positive … meanwhile i was doing a very stupid thing … i was going to a a meetings where the probationers were attending … the judge of the court i reported to sent half of them there … if there were thirty in a meeting twenty five were sent in there by the judge … and to cap it off i shared things in these meetings that those criminals should have never heard … totally nutzy …

… i have to agree with that … no really … even i can tell that was not a good idea …

… i had no problem doing the work . the problem was relationships with the people on the street … key west is a small community and it was not long before folks around town knew i was a cop … and stayed away from me …

… did you carry a gun …

… in the academy we went through firearms training but the department left it up to us to carry … i decided not to …

... why ... you were dealing with a bunch of criminals ...

... i knew the trouble guns can get you into in law enforcement ... every officer on the dallas force that got involved in a shooting got sued and investigated for a crime ... i do not like guns ... and i had no reason to go around pulling one on someone ... i had very little contact with the probationers out of the a a meetings and i only checked on a few at their residence ... if they had a residence ... i only checked on a few every month ...

... did any of the other officers carry a gun ...

... a few did but most of us did not ...

... so you admitted to being an alcoholic and being bipolar and you were given a gun if you wanted one ...

... yeah ... and i was insane ...

... did you go home at all ...

... no i just hanged around the island ... but in a few weeks i ... well let me tell you ... when i was standing on a bridge over a ... dock just walking around ... well i saw this ray ... i thought it would be neat to see these guys face to face ... i went out to the naval base and checked out the snorkel gear ... they had a whole department filled with scuba gear ... that sort of turned me on ... i got the idea to try that ... but i needed to know what i needed ... so i drove back onto the island and stopped at the first dive shop i came to ... i got lined up with a scuba course ... i used their rental equipment until i found out if i could do it or not ... thus i started on my new found hobby of scuba diving ... but the first dive i made was in the local pool where us new guys took our training ... i could afford all this with my retirement and all ... to tell you the truth i would not have taken the job if i did not have my half of the retirement ...

... your half ...

... yeah my wife and i split it down the middle ...

... why do you say that you would not have taken the job ...

... it paid twenty four a year ...

... twenty four thousand a year and you needed a degree ... lord ...

... hey it was florida ... so i lived pretty good even in key west ... i started diving on the weekends and sometimes made four dives ...

two each day … i built up a lot of dive time quickly and moved on to the advanced course …

… *you must have been a good swimmer* …

… you do not need to know how to swim to scuba dive … but i was a good swimmer and was in real good shape after the academy … we would go to sunken boats and look at the fish … each of the wrecks had a moray eel and a jew fish …

… *moray eels* …

… yes … you can pet them they are so friendly … and barracuda are friendly too … you cannot pet them but they will follow you around like a little puppy …

… *i thought they were dangerous* …

… the folks that make the movies want you to believe that… there were two things i did not like being around … one was jelly fish and the other …

… *was sharks* …

… you got it … they are like dobermans … you have no idea what they are going to do … the bull sharks are the worst … they will slam into you to stun you … the sharks were just something you had to put up with … they made me real anxious … anyway … i went on from advanced to dive master … i was really proud of myself …

… *it was kind of an extension of flying and jumping was it not* …

… i looked at it that way … scuba diving was getting to be my only pleasurable thing to do … work was now falling down on me … my medication was tearing me up … i probably had too much in my system … i asked the psych i was seeing what was the problem and all he would reply was that i was crazy and laugh … i did not trust him at all … he was a sleaze … but he was the only one that would take my insurance and the naval base had no psychiatrist … i thought that by this time i should have been put on something else … the medication was just not working … actually it was making me worse … it was noticed at work and i was overcome with the feelings of being caught …

… *again* …

… yep … that was the cycle … take a good job … let my anxiety destroy me and quit … i did quit … i resigned with only seven months on the job … i knew i was a joke around the office and the supervisors hated me … one went to an a a meeting with me and ratted me out … the boss told me i could no longer go to meetings … i went off the deep end and became a shut in except for the scuba diving … it was not long before i was back in the hospital … a clinic run by the same jerk doctor that overloaded me on the medication … i committed myself and could not leave … i was behind locked doors … out of some demented interest a few from the office came to visit me …

… i was kept in the clinic with absolutely nothing to do except read and watch t v … i did not watch t v because i did not want to spend time with the other patients … several of the staff asked me why i was in there and it dawned on me that the doctor was dipping very deeply into my insurance … i got on the phone and told my insurance company what he was doing and i was released the next day …they cut him off … i walked out of the place and threw my meds away … i actually started to feel better in a few days … as good as a bipolar without medication can feel …

… i just hung around the apartment through the week and then dove on the weekends … then one weekend someone … i forget who … someone in the dive shop quit and they needed someone to work in the dive shop and store … i told them i could … they hired me on the spot and paid me minimum wage … i went from twenty four grand a year to ten thousand … hey with my retirement i could live off it … i worked in the shop during the week and then dove on the weekend with the tourists … i was paid to dive as a dive master … it was a bit of a stretch but i was a professional diver … i was working about sixty hours a week and going to a a meetings … that was my life in the spring of ninety four … then a life changing event happened … i know i sound dramatic … but for a bipolar off meds it was all drama …

… the owners of the shop had a daughter … she was thirteen and wanted to get into a summer drama program … but like ninety percent of actors she was afraid to audition … she did not know how … there was a central casting off ice in key west … not casting really … it was for bookings for bands and acts as key west was replete with bars … i called and asked if any plays were in town or if they could put me in touch with a director that would spare me a little time … as luck would have it they were casting a play and were auditioning the next day … now this is one of those comet out of the sky events …

… go on …

… so i take her to the audition and talk to the director about what i am doing … i asked if he would let me audition before her so i could show her what to do … he said he was glad to accommodate … although none of the parts were right for a thirteen year old he let us perform … then out of the kindness of his heart he gave us a call back for the next day … so back we went … but this time we were asked to fill out audition cards … she auditioned first this time and then i went on … i thanked him for his kindness and we left … the next day he called and told me he had cast me in the lead … and it was a legitimate play …

… a what …

… i would be getting paid for it …

… ah so …

… this was right down the old bipolar alley …

… let me guess … something to look forward to …

… sal you are so wise …

... to be or not to be a thesbian ...

... we had a read through of the play the evening after we were cast
... it was six of us ... the play was nineteen fifty nine pink cadillac ...
it was two plays back to back ... the first was laundry and bourbon
with three woman ... two of which were married to two of the three
men in the second play called lone star ... i was to play an alcoholic
cowboy and viet nam vet .... it was not a stretch ... i loved the part
as it was well written and the characters were more important than
the plot ... the plot for both plays was that we were all flawed ... i
could not wait for rehearsals and when the play date came i was more
ready for the part than any other role i had ever played ... we were
all pros with experience and it showed in the performances ... we
got rave reviews from all four of the newspapers in town ... it is easy
to believe your reviews when they are good ... in reality the ticket
sales were the review ... what the papers said helped us a little ...
but it was word of mouth that filled up the seats ... the plays had a
two week run and when i walked away from the theater after the last
performance i was full of pride ... i had done something that i did not
feel as though i would be caught and quit ... for the first time in my
life i felt competent ...

... in your whole life ...

... yes that is how deep the feelings were ... how ingrained my
self loathing was ... but not that night ... i still remember it ... when
i look back on my life i have a hard time keeping the downers out ...
the misery i caused to myself and others ... but that night walking
away from the waterfront theater was a triumph ... and i decided to
continue with it ... the acting i mean ... that night i decided i would

go to new york city and give acting a good try … i owed it to myself … so i packed my stuff in a trailer … a very small trailer … i did not have that much … said goodbye to a few people i knew and went on my way … i did stop off to see my wife … i never asked her what she thought of the idea … i knew i had to move on …

… i made a few phone calls to apartment brokers in the city and had some contacts … i also had saved enough money that with my retirement i could live for a year without working … with my retirement coming in that is … i pulled in to fort hamilton in brooklyn of the second of july of ninety four … in the last year i had been a probation officer … a resident in a mental clinic and a scuba divemaster and now a professional actor … i stayed in the guest quarters for a few nights … the next day i got a map of the city with the subway systems on it and went to a brokers address in the bronx … the subway was an adventure and i got off on the same block as the brokers office … i took one look around and walked across the street and got back on the southbound train … the bronx looked like berlin in forty five … it looked like a bombed out mess with storefronts boarded up and street people all over the place … no thanks … cheap rent or not i was not staying there … i did know that manhattan would be too expensive … so i thought i would try brooklyn … i got back to fort hamilton in the afternoon and decided to try the next day forgetting it was the fourth of july … i went to the club to get something to eat and was not allowed in …

… how is that …

… i had my identification card but the manager … a mean and nasty german told me i would have to bring in my military record for her to review … it was the last time i went into the club … jews do not take well to pain in the butt germans … i told her in german that she was out of line before i left … it shocked her to get her own stuff back … i accented the words as though it was coming direct from the reich … i stood up for myself … which was an unusual event for me … the confidence from the play in key west was sticking with me … i guess i could have intimidated her into letting me stay … but no matter what … i do not go where i am not wanted … i hold to that today ... back then it was pride ... now it is avoidance of conflict but a lot more of that later ...

... so ... where was i ...

... looking for a place to live in brooklyn ...

... on the morning of the fourth i decided to take a walk and see what was in the neighborhood ... a few blocks up the street i came upon an apartment brokers office and it was open ... there was a lady in the rear of the office going through some paperwork ... i asked her if they had anything ... her first question was to ask my name and introduce herself ... the second question was how much i could afford ... ah ... an open and shut case as to the criteria ... she got me a cup of coffee and told me she had everything from rooms for a couple of hundred bucks to three bedroomers for two grand a month ... i did not want a room but did not need a big place ... she said she had two efficiency apartments for five hundred a month utilities and cable included ... that was better than my key west apartment ... and she added the apartments were only a few blocks away ... she told me she could show me the places in the morning ...

... first thing we got to it ... i drove ... i soon came to realize the last thing i needed was a car in the city ... we may as well have walked as the parking space we found was just as far away as fort hamilton ... the first place was a walkup that did not have its own bathroom ... but the second place was perfect ... it was about the size of half a racket ball court with a kitchenette and a shower ... it was going to be tight ... i had three tall shelve sets and a hundred books or so ... why i carried those books around i do not know ... well i did not know at the time ... i later realized i was hanging on to the past and the books were the only thing that was mine ... that i felt were really mine ... i took the place and moved in the next day ...

... i went to a newsstand up the street and inquired if there were any publications pertaining to show business ... agents and auditions and casting ... he handed me a copy of backstage and said it comes out every week ... i rushed home with it after buying a map of manhattan to plot out all the acting studios and audition halls and rehearsal halls listed in the paper ...

… it was a military project …

… an operations order was it …

… almost … i located all those places and plotted them on the map … after which i set about a route to walk to each one of them in order in the shortest route … i also looked up auditions posted for the next week … i had to set a goal for weekly and monthly auditions … i set it for at least six a week and thirty for the month … i knew auditions were a numbers game …

… kind of like a sales quota …

… exactly … i also thought that to get started i would take whatever i could get … whether it paid or not i would take the first thing that came along … after that only paying jobs … although i knew some of them would be contingent upon the film making money … i was not too interested in doing plays but if it paid … well okay …

… but the first thing that monday i went down the street to a temp agency and filled out an application … i knew i would have a lot of time on my hands and i may as well do some clerical work somewhere … i got back to my apartment before i started off on my studios trek and the temp agency called and offered me a full time job running the office … i of course turned them down … they never called me for a temp job … anyway off i went to greenwich village and on course to meet as many people as i could and give them a photo and resume … i put everything i did on my resume but i was up front and listed the speaking parts first … i wanted to give them the idea of honestly …

… did you think you would be dishonest … that sounds like a weird question …

… give you an example of some of the things actors do especially the kids … if they read a bit of mcbeth in drama school they will put down they played mcbeth … if they are in a student project they will list it as a feature film … so a lot of twenty years olds have full resumes … the casting directors can see right through it …

… i however had a lot of training in film and had done some films… college kids are taught very bad drama by cannot doers …

… cannot doers … enlighten me …

… if you can … do … if you cannot … teach … do not get me wrong there are doers and teachers but generally not in colleges …

… ah … get it …

… my age was a plus … i was forty eight … so i could play between thirty five and fifty five … plus i had hair back then … i also knew that on film i looked menacing … i was a heavy … a character actor … but i auditioned for everything that came along … and i planned to do the same in new york …

… the end of the first day i had met and talked with about ten directors and casting agents that were also running studios for classes … now let me separate the studio instruction from the college classroom … the folks that teach in the studios are working performers and directors … not so in schools …

… i did not want to get involved in any schools until i got the lay of the land … why spend the money if you are going to work … and the second day i got an audition at the fifty fourth street theater … it was for a play … a greek tragedy called philoctetes by sophacles … i ended up with the lead the next day but it was a no payer … i read about an audition for a film and went to it on that friday … on saturday i was called and offered the costarring role as the coach of a college soccer team … the film was called snapshots from a five hundred season … it was a coming of age film about college kids … it paid twelve hundred dollars … as the play was not fully cast and we had not even had a read through … i backed out of it and made a pledge to myself to not take anything that did not pay unless it benefited my resume and did not create a scheduling conflict with other roles … in essence i was to be paid or no film or play … it was an extreme move for me to do that … me of little confidence … but i was riding high … i also thought that this business of acting cannot be all that bad if i got a good role within a week …

… but twelve hundred dollars was not much …

… oh but it was for an independent film … and i did not even have an agent … this is where the two films i made in dallas … one called demon warrior and the second brutal fury … this is where i knew i had the experience to feel confident … plus i was doing something that since i was eight years old wanted to do … i was in the movie business … filming began in about three weeks so i had time to go to other auditions … my goal was six a week … sometimes i did four or five in one day … and the good thing about auditions is you only remember the last one and you do not sit around fretting about getting the part …

… i auditioned for everything … plays and t v and commercials and print media and of course movies … a lot of the roles were not right for me …

… so why audition …

… very good question … i auditioned because the directors would move on to other things and hopefully they would remember me the next time i showed up … i was offered roles but turned them down because they did not pay …

… while i was filming snapshots i got a role in a short subject that was being used to garner money for a feature … the cast was betting on the short film titled hungreed to sell the feature … this was a case where it was worth it to me to take the chance … as it turned out the short subject was very good but we never got the stake money to do the feature … what the hey i took a chance …

… actually going to any audition was taking a chance that i may get the part … i got a part as a dragon in a chinese theater production but i was to sick with the flu to take it … i feel i really missed out on a good experience … but sick is sick …

… i also did have a lot of down time and to fill the voids i signed up with two temp companies … one was for convention staff and the other was a catering company … i got some work and made a few extra bucks … it gave me a little mad money in case i got the urge …

… the urge … the urge to do what …

… oh buy something … see a show … that brings up another good point … i never went to broadway shows … i went to theaters in greenwich village … it was more my level at the time … you cannot get into major productions without major league representation … that … more often than not is what determines who gets the part … it is like the difference between a good lawyer and a public defender …

... after a month or two i got an agent ... she was not union and charged fifteen percent of the parts she got me ... she was a lovely person but bless her heart she never got me a part ... i would check in with her every now and then but nothing ever came of it ... i got my own work by following audition leads and word of mouth ...

... the best break i got in the city was for a play believe it or not ... i do not like plays ... i think most of them are weak ... but i went to the audition and found out the staff in west palm beach florida was in a bind ... the story was that the first two actors that had the part backed out ... and they needed to cast it then and there ... i had an idea i would get it ... i was right for the part ... i could do the eastern european accent and was a quick study ... the play had two people in it ... was sixty three pages of dialog and there was no intermission ... i should have been suspicious ... but i forged ahead as it paid pretty well ... i ended up getting forty seven hundred dollars for it but had to pay my own lodging and food ...

... i flew to west palm beach and within five minutes of meeting the producer understood why the first two actors had quit ...

... that bad ...

... oh the guy was a complete noodnik ...

... noodnik ...

... neurotic ... neurotic and full of himself ... he actually thought he was going to produce his stuff on broadway ... i was actually afraid i was not going to be paid ... the play was tallys folly and was a real tough drama ... a real tough story of lost love and tortured backgrounds ... it was not a comedy ...

... i found out the tickets had been sold based upon a t v star taking the role ... i thought to myself ... this is not going to be received very well by the audiences ... it was in a jewish community center and all the performances were of a jewish theme which tallys folly was ... my costar had a lot more stage experience than me and she did not mind telling me about it ... i felt lost and went into a real funk ... i rehearsed the lines over and over and got them down in ten days ... the setting was first class and i felt i had a lot of responsibility to the crew to make this all come off … and i pulled it off even though i was very depressed … but the part called for me to be depressed …

… we ran for two weeks and i was glad to see the curtain come down … i vowed to never take a play again unless it paid so much i could not turn away from it … it was a completely mercenary attitude on my part …

… the biggest benefit of doing the play was that it earned me a union card … i could now audition at the actors equity union hall … so it was worth the time and extreme effort to my brain … but if i had to mark my downturn in new york it was when i returned from tallys folly … i was back to my ups and downs … i had day player roles in two films … too much sleep and sleepy heads … i also got a role for two episodes of loving the soap opera …

… did you get paid much for day player roles …

… couple of hundred … then i got the biggest most important role of my film career … it was called backroad diner and i played this whacko cop … when i was in the scene i owned it … the screenplay for my role was the best i had ever seen … i even got kudos at the cannes film festival … it was the hallmark of my stay in new york … i loved the part … i fit it so well and it was the third time i died in a picture … the first two were the films in dallas …

… do you have a list of your films …

… on my headshot and resume … but you can google me … seriously they are all listed … but i got the idea that … well let me explain it this way … in the rehearsal hall of the union was a large lobby and these old timers sat around and talked about the good old days when they almost got a part and what could have been … i got honest with myself and decided i did not want to be like that … i felt i was playing first string in the minor leagues but i was not going to be called to the majors … i had interviewed with agents but none seemed interested … so i had a string of independent films … the real work was in the union movies … and with the exception of a very small role in dallas in a film called trapped and some work on dallas in dallas i had not seen much union action …

… so what was your decision …

… well i was torn …

… how so …

… i was a sponsor to three twelve steppers and felt i was helping them …

… from a a …

… nope from overeaters anonymous …

… you were overweight …

… no i was just looking to belong to something and going to twelve step meetings was my way of feeling i was part of something … i also went to a a meetings but then i had a glass of wine at a restaurant and felt i did not belong there as i had failed …

… why did you drink a glass of wine if you felt you needed to be in a a …

… i knew i was not an alcoholic … just listening to the other stories told me i did not have a drinking problem … what i had was a behavior problem …

… did you have any behavior issues that you had not mentioned before …

… well … i would lie on my futon in my little apartment for days on end … i would get all cranked up for auditions … i was swinging from one extreme to the other …

… that is bipolar is it not …

… i did not see it that way … i felt that if i could just control my emotions i would be all right and that my depression and mania was a problem with control … i was not on meds at the time … however it was in new york where i started not to blame others and hoped that they would shape up but i started to blame myself … if i would just shape up … i think i had the wherewithal to grade myself and others … probably brought on by my realizing that my acting was not leading anywhere …

… maybe that was a plus for you …

… what it did though was have me look at myself as more of a failure … i asked to come back to florida to try to get something else … i had no idea what i was going to do … my wife let me come back to live there … but before i leave new york in this discussion let me tell you about two events …

… i was in my apartment one sunday night and a weekly news magazine show came on … the reporter started out her piece that she called a one eight hundred number to a mental health clinic and was asked what she was calling about … she told the person on the other end … a psychologist … that she was depressed … he set her up for a ticket to his clinic …

… that was all the information he got from her … he made an evaluation that she was merely depressed …

… yes … sound familiar … so i stopped what i was doing and watched and low and behold her crew showed up at the same clinic i had gone to … as it turned out after the news piece they closed their doors … it seems that the doctors of psychology were not … the social workers were not … the whole thing was an insurance scam just like the clinic i was in down in key west …

… you were diagnosed and treated for bipolar based on that information … information from scam artists …

… yes the question was now …

… were you bipolar …

… exactly … the doctor that treated me was a doctor … he was later jammed up in court … go figure … my question was … am i truly bipolar … i believed i was … i thought he was right in my case … it did not matter what the malady was … i was on no meds …

… then i talked to a social worker in key west … just a friendly call … it turned out that my supervisor with the probation office was brought up on charges for extorting money from the probationers … she ended up doing five years …

… okay let be get this straight … in dallas your chief of police got busted and fired … in new hampshire your director of security got fired for records tampering and now in key west your boss goes down for five years …

… not a good record of choosing jobs …

… sounds like it …

… or it was just the nature of the beast for arrogant people to seek promotion and positions of power … like they thought they would not get caught … or thought they were too powerful for the system to come down on them …

  … so on to florida …

  … and another adventure …

... breaker breaker ...

... i got down there in september of ninety five and started looking once again ... i had a good run in new york and took pride in the fact that i had done more in a year than most had done in their whole career ... also i was in the five percent of actors that made a living acting ... but that was all behind me now ...

... so what did you do ...

... i interviewed for some corrections jobs but did not hear from them ... and then came upon an ad in the newspaper for a truck driving school ... i thought i may want to try that ... i had heard from the drivers i knew that they made very good money ... whatever very good money was ... so off i went and spent over three thousand for the school ...

... i took to it very easily and got the idea that i could just stay on the road ... i got a job with a national company and was put into their training program ... i would drive with another driver ... a trainer for about six weeks ... we were on the road for about an hour and he let me drive ... i guess he got the idea that i was not going to flip it over and from then on we worked as partners ... what i was learning from him was all the things i would need to get me started ...

... oh ... i did get a corrections job offer but i was already committed to the truck driving ... and in the state i was in it was good for me to just be alone ... after six weeks i was turned loose and started to drive all over the east coast ... i asked to go west to visit my daughter in dallas ... i would stay out on the road for two months at a time ... but let me tell you it was not good pay ... i was clearing about three fifty a week ...

... what ... i thought you got paid on miles ... did you not drive a lot of miles ...

... okay ... true you are paid on miles but not road miles ... map miles ... if i delivered in atalnta say in midtown i was not paid for the miles i drove but only to the outskirts of atlanta ... it was a rip off but that was the business ... so any hoopla you hear about truckers making that good money ... at the most forty a year ... even today the new drivers are only making twenty eight or so ... it is considered unskilled labor ... and really you just do the same thing over and over ... pick up a load here and deliver it there ...

... sounds kind of boring ...

... it can be ... but i listed to three audio books a day and i read while i was waiting to be loaded or unloaded ... plus i got paid extra if i did my own loading and unloading ... it helped to keep me in shape ... and besides you can drive whether you are depressed or not ... i was given this book by this social worker i knew in key west ... we met at an al anon meeting ...

... of course ...

... anyway it was the best book i have ever read ... it gave me a new perspective on so many things ...

... like ...

... things religious things spiritual things new age ...

... can you give me the name of the book ...

... i guess so ... it is called conversations with god by neale donald walsch ... i read it ... oh probably ten times while on the road ... it is one of those books that gives you more each time you read it ... the biggest lesson i got from it was that ... follow me ... in the absence of that which we are not that which we are is not ...

... whoa ... let me think of that for a minute ...

... now that is not original ... it was just that it was explained to me better than most new ideas ... it was not original for new agers but it was new for me ... i can put it in a bipolar context ... without depression i could not know mania ... without happiness one cannot know sadness ... if i was manic all the time i could not appreciate it as i had nothing to measure it by ... but in the context of the book was the idea of magnificence and that which was not magnificent ... god could not know the wonder of it all until god created that which was not positive ... the fall in the garden gave god and us that which was not magnificent ...

... therefore you can experience the good side of things by experiencing the bad side of things ... mania versus depression ...

... absolutely ... when i latched on to that one thought ... that one idea ... well i was able to cope with myself ... i was not getting any better but at least i could look at myself as not being a total wreck ... i was bipolar ... not on meds ... but understood the condition better than ever before ...

. as a trucker i had very little to do with others ... getting bills of laity signed ... ordering meals in truck stops ... i could go whole days without saying more than ten words a day ... drive ... drink coffee ... listen to audio books ... read and sleep in the rear of the cab ... it was a good life for me at the time ... and i was coming around to the idea that i could cure myself by a change in behavior ... and being an uncommunicative trucker was the change ...

... that was not too healthy was it ... you were completely alone ...

... except when i made visits to my daughter in dallas ... i visited my wife a couple of times also ... i did not however visit new york or key west ...

... i was at the headquarters of the company waiting for a load and heard that they needed an in house trainer ... i thought it over and decided it was time for me to venture out in the world with my new found behavior ...

... and what did you feel was the biggest behavior change ...

... not being too outgoing and not saying off the wall things ... i tried to think myself through the condition of making my world what i was thinking ... i thought strange thoughts but i tried not to articulate them ... it was easy to hold myself in check when there was no one else around ... hey ... you can think anything when you are alone and you can say anything when there is no one there to talk to ... i thought i was altering my behavior but in essence i was just living away from the element that made me realize my mistakes ... i had no society to deal with … what i was doing was fooling myself … also … i showed my lack of self worth when i talked to them about taking the job … they asked me how much i would work for … i low balled the offer and told management i would do it for twenty four a year …

… *low ball … i should say … why did you give them such a low figure …*

… one i was sure i would get the job with an offer like that … and two i felt that was all the job was worth … what i was worth …

… *were you not getting into the same mindset as you did with jobs before …*

… precisely … i was kidding myself that i could cure this thing called bipolar … i was right back where i started …

… *what exactly was the job …*

… i trained the new employees on the system and policies of the company … plus they took a comprehensive road test with the company … i taught everything from map reading to how we kept our logs … it was a good administrative job … i would go in early and get set up for each days instruction … we had the new employees there for a week so i taught from monday to friday … the weekends were spent in my apartment alone … i was back to watching t v and playing on my computer … i had a laptop that i used as a word processor … i wrote a lot … i edited a book i wrote in bolivia … it gave me something to do … then i found unity …

… *you united with yourself … please explain …*

… no … what i am talking about is unity church …

… *i am not familiar with unity …*

… the best way i can explain it is that it is new age … it followed the book i told you about … the one i read ten times … i also asked for a divorce … she agreed with all the provisions and i was single for the first time in twenty eight years …

… *provisions …*

… yes … i gave her half my retirement and the house … it was only fair as she did not have the opportunity to establish anything for herself while we were in the military … moving around all the time

… plus i felt guilty about the way my illness affected me and how that affected her …

… at work i was beginning to get the old feeling of being found out … plus the place was in financial trouble … that coupled with my boss trying to fire his whole department …

… huh …

… yep he wanted to fire all of his safety staff and start over … he would have had no one working for him … he was nuts and he was removed from the position … but they did not fire him … i was real insecure by now … it was then i decided to go to beauty school …

… another huh …

… i left the company on an angry manic episode …

… explain please …

… essentially there are two types of manic states … the exuberant periods of doing and doing … that is why a lot of bipolars are so educated … or in show business … exuberance … but there is also the dark side of mania and that is the rages … i think as you get older the rages come on …

… but beauty school … why that …

… i had a little experience with it from my aunts shop … i have no idea as to why i chose that … i just did … i was in a state of complete confusion … but went ahead with enrolling in the school … i was also getting more active in unity … truth be known unity was not very good for me … plus i was a jew and unity was a christian fellowship as the term goes … what the hey … when in rome … right …

… how do you mean active …

… we put on a talent show and i had a lot of fun with that … i also met this guy i hit it off with … and i also met my second wife … i was seeing her as i was going through beauty school … she had a pet grooming shop and was at one time a hairdresser herself … she had a son that had a family and a daughter with some emotional and learning problems which was to be a problem for us in the future …

… i finished beauty school and started to work in a shop in muncie … i lasted six weeks and i was out of a job … seven thousand for beauty school and i hated it … i felt everyone i worked on was disapproving of me … i did not realize that hairdressing paid zilch and was complaint city … how do you want your hair cut … i do not know … well tell me how long you like to wear it … i do not know … okay … the next thing out of her mouth was i do not like the cut … she did not know what she wanted but what she got was not it …

… not it what …

… not what she wanted …

… but she did not know what she wanted …

… now you got it …

… anyway my future wife had her bather quit … so the groom shop was short a vital element … i told her i would bathe the dogs and cats for her … after all i was out of a job …

… i started bathing the animals and soon she was teaching me how to groom … i had no problem with the implements as i was a hairdresser and soon took to the work … each breed has a specific cut so i had to learn the designs … if i did not know the cut there was a book i could get the design from … all i had to do was look at the picture of the dogs finished cut and could do it … i soon realized that i was getting all the cats that came in … no one liked to work with them … have you ever shampooed or blow dried a cat …

… cannot say as i have …

… it is like handling a fish in the bottom of the boat … but unlike fish the cats tend to bite … so i got cat bit all the time … i got dog bit also … it just went along with the trade … now it was not an everyday thing … but the bites came often enough … soon we hired another bather and i was cutting hair on my own … pet grooming is the most money i have ever made … it is much more lucrative than cutting the hair of the undecided …

… allow me to digress … what i write about others and the situations i got myself into was in the throes of the bipolar disorder … i know i talked about this a bit before … i am trying my best to give you the mindset of how i was at the time …

… we got married and i moved in … but i was going downhill fast … i could handle the dogs and cats and the shop administration …

but i could not handle my off time … i lost interest in everything but v h one …

… *v h one … the video channel ...*

… yes i was obsessed with it … i spent half a day watching boy george specials … i could not get enough of music videos …

… *what did your new wife have to say about the v h one bit ...*

… not much she was busy with a second business … i was running the shop and we had three other groomers … the place looked great as over the holidays i redid the whole design of the shop … it looked like a beauty salon … styling stations and mirrors … we got new equipment at a pet grooming show and were really getting to be uptown … it was the winter of ninety nine … that december … december of ninety eight we went to wisconsin to my daughters wedding … she married a pilot from my old regiment in germany … he was stationed in tucson arizona … i got to walk her down the aisle … it was a very good day and i behaved myself quite well … but … and a big but … i was becoming less than high functional … the description of me at the clinic in california … i was beginning to feel the bipolar … it encroached upon me … i was souring emotionally … i felt trapped …

… *trapped in the marriage ...*

… no … no … i felt trapped in my head … i could not get away from my own racing thoughts … i could not get away from the cycling … the constant torment … i was docile … i was not in rage mania … yet … i decided to take a step towards getting help …

… i went down to the emergency room of the hospital in anderson indiana where i was living … my wife thought it was a good idea … so off i go … i check in at the emergency room and was told to go across the street to the mental health clinic … i checked in there and in about an hour was told to go back to the emergency room … so over i go and sit there for about an hour and then i was told to go back to the mental health clinic and see a nurse … a practitioner that could prescribe meds … ah … at least someone was paying attention to me … finally … i told her about my bipolar diagnoses and that there were no records to retrieve … the clinic in california had nothing on me … she had heard about the scam … she however … i believe … no …

i know she misinterpreted my mania … my mania to be depression and prescribed an antidepressant … she told me to check back in two weeks to see if the meds kicked in …

… i went away with some confidence as at least i had taken some action and the anderson clinic did not feel like the scam i had gone through in california and the insurance racket i had experienced in key west … i was able to calm down a bit but i believe it was my belief in the meds and not necessarily the meds themselves …

… the noise in my head was back … so what did she do … she prescribed another antidepressant on top of the one i was taking … in two weeks i was somewhat agitated … i thought it was a phase i was going through to have the meds kick in … i went back in two weeks …

… she considered me not to be at the level she wanted me to be … i told her something i had read about bipolar and that i wanted to get to where i was playing between the thirty five yard lines … i was playing upfield in the mania range on the twenty yard line and felt i was getting worse … so what does she do … she prescribes a third antidepressant for me … i became real agitated and also became very dopey … i became tired and restless and began to feel rage inside … it had not come out yet but it was on the surface … in two weeks i was back down to see her and had very rapid speech and the shakes … i explained how i felt on the meds … she put me on the most popular antidepressant on the market …

… she prescribed it on top on the other three antidepressants …

… indeed she did and after one day i became so paranoid i stayed under a table in my wifes massage room for four days … i was afraid of everything … i ate nothing and the only water i drank was to take my meds … i went from internal rage to paranoia to listlessness as i became more weakened by the meds … i was a mess to say the least …

… i also felt a lot of guilt because of burdening my wife with the basket case i had become … she seemed to take it well … she was however on the verge of putting me in the hospital … i had finally gotten out from under the table but was in no state of mind to work

… i felt useless and weak … but i will give the meds the due … i was not raging internally … i was not thinking much at all … i say looking back on it that i was over the goal line on the mania side … i was a blank …

… do you not think you were depressed …

… no … looking back … no i do not …my mania … my rage mania had just been dulled but the nurse thought i was depressed and when she found out the under the table bit just exchanged that antidepressant for another … i came out of her office still on four antidepressants … and then the rages started … i could not control the screaming and yelling … my voice became hoarse and i would create very bad headaches for myself … this was the worst i had ever been … i actually hoped i would feel bad enough to get back under the table …

… what did you rage against …

… nothing in particular … i would just scream … i would just get excited and angry … i thought i was falling apart in these tantrums … i never thought it was the meds … one night it got so bad i was taken down to the police station … i had to go to court the next morning and pleaded guilty … that was an embarrassment …

… guilty of what …

… i do not know … whatever the judge said … i was fined twenty five dollars and made to go to a church program …

… was it domestic violence …

… no … it was disturbing the peace … there is no record of it … the judge must have made it a fine of no record … i got another cop job later on and it did not pop up on the background check … so it was no big deal …

… wait a minute … the judge sent you to a church program … that kind of violates the separation of church and state does it not …

… yeah … i thought of that sometime after the fact … but i went to the program and to this day do not know what it was all about … to tell you the truth i do not even remember it … even though i was involved in unity and the church program i was not spiritual enough …

*... hold on ... how did that come about ... who measures spirituality
...*

... my wife and the other coowners of the healing business they
started up ... it was five of them in all ... but they judged their
husbands not on the same spiritual plane as they were ...

... oh for heavens sake ...

... i also decided that the meds were not working and for three days
weaned myself off the drugs ... all four of them ... i told my nurse
and she got me in to see a psychiatrist ... she considered what i did a
very bad move ... but i was off the stuff when i went to see the psych
... i had my wife and her daughter in to see him and the daughter was
very angry and wanted me out of the house ... she wanted me gone ...

... what did your wife say ...

... nothing ... i got no defense from her ... but the psych put me on
another medication ... another antidepressant ...

... the rages came back ...

... i was dull ... cycling and angry ... and i started the yelling
behavior again ... only i did it mostly when i was alone ... i did not
want the cops there again ... i was lucid enough to figure that out ...
being the fifth husband ...

*... whoa ... wait ... the fifth husband ... your wife had been married
four times before ...*

... no ... i was the fifth husband to be put upon because i was not
spiritual enough ... i was given all sorts of new age books to read to
get my life straightened out ... they said the same thing ...

... and what was that ...

... they all told me that the writer walked in the light of perfection
and i was a shmuck ... i could not fake being anything but what i was
... the books just made me feel worse about myself ... i called them
feel good books ... i knew one thing i had to get away from the mess
... i had to get out of the marriage ... i had left two times before but
just went to a motel for a few days ... some nights i would sleep in
my truck ... but this time i had to go ... i was mentally ill ... in a rage
... overwhelmed in my mania and was spirituality lacking ... the last
one had no fix ... even the minister at the unity church thought i was

lacking spiritually … she even threatened me physically if i did not shape up …

… threatened you physically … how so …

… she wanted to slap my face … i was very confused … the minister of my church did not want me there … how low can you go …

… what about a a …

… no need to go there … you think i was going to drink anything on top of the meds …

… so i just packed up my stuff in a rental trailer and off i went … i asked my daughter if i could stay with her for a few days … i was homeless and on my way to tucson … i had no idea what was in store for me … but i had gotten away … the fifth husband was gone …

… all the others left their wives also …

… everyone of them … i was the fifth and last …

… weird … just plain new age weird …

… i guess that is what you could call it … i started on the journey by going to the psychiatrists office and saying goodbye … i had an appointment that morning … he was happy to see me get away … i was still on the one antidepressant … and for the four day journey i fasted … took in nothing except water and coffee … had to have coffee … i got stuck in an ice storm in texas so it took me five days … nothing for an ex trucker … as a matter of fact that is what i would be doing … trucking …

... the devil at the door ...

... oh let us try truck driving again ... that is what i did when i moved to tucson ... i did not want to just sit around my daughters house ... i wanted to get out and do something ... i had broken free of the spiritual spiral ... i had broken free from the drugs that caused my rage ... i had broken free from a marriage that was an absolute disaster ... so me getting on the road was the best answer ... i would be alone again ... i could deal with myself on the borderline of a meltdown ... but once out on the road i just went from place to place ... listened to audio books and read ... but in six months i was sick of it ...

... one of the few times i stopped in tucson i applied to have my cosmetology license transferred from indiana to arizona ... i came through in may and i decided to leave a driving job that was about two fifty a week in my pocket ... yeah ... that was all ... things are worse than florida in the grand canyon state ... i figured i could make that cutting hair part time ... so i quit the trucking business for good ... i promised myself i would never go back ... and i have not ...

... my daughter and son in law were away and i was house sitting ... it gave me a good break and i had no pressure to find a place of my own ... while i was taking care of their place i got an apartment and bought some furniture ... i was no longer homeless ... i took my time ... i work best when there is no pressure ...

... it was the memorial day weekend when i decided to go downtown to see what was up with tucson ... i asked someone somewhere where to go for the holiday and was told fourth avenue ... i got there and went into a coffee shop ... but as i entered the shop i saw a sign outside a bar that advertized a cabaret show ... it was to take place at two that afternoon ... i decided to go ... it was whacky ... it was a drag show ... now i had been introduced to drag shows in indiana by a friend that took me to a gay pride day fair ... i had never seen anything like it and thought drag shows were a hoot ... i still do although i have not attended one in years ... anyway i went into the show and it blew me away ... it was upscale compared to indiana ... an act from vegas was there ...

... now let us put this in perspective ... i was not on meds ... i was all alone in a strange city ... i am not gay and i started going to drag shows ... i thought ... what the hey ... maybe ... just maybe ... i would fit in ...

... that weekend i stopped into a salon ... one of those franchise shops ... in the hairdressing business they are called chop shops ... i wanted to talk to the manager about what was going on with the business in tucson ... she hired me on the spot ... well ... one shop is as good as the other ... so i signed on ... my apartment was across the street ... i was also out of transportation ... i had sold my truck while i was truck driving ... i did not want to see it sit for months in the company parking lot ... it was a dumb thing to do ... i practically gave it away ... and now i had no wheels ... but i had a good deal of money saved up and had no bills except for the apartment ... i could have lived there off my retirement ... but it would have been close ... besides ... what was i going to do ... just sit around ... so i went out and bought a car and was set up with a job a ride and an apartment ... i was doing real well or so i thought ... in no time at all i was forcing myself to get through the work day ... i was only working about thirty hours a week ... i was making about three hundred a week clear ... not really that bad for a basket case ... i would throw myself on my futon and lie there in desperation ... i became so angry at myself for feeling the way i did i would beat myself on the head ... i bruised my temples so much that it hurt just to turn my head ...

... at work i told them i would work any hours they liked ... the only thing i asked for was to get off on thursday nights so i could go to the drag shows ... after awhile they got to know me at the club ... it was great to have someone notice me ... the drag shows and the video

store across the street from my apartment were my entertainment …
i would see my daughter about once every two weeks … she was
starting to worry about me … i was going to drag shows had several
earrings hanging down from my ears and made no sense what so ever
…

… i stayed with that shop for about ten months … until i got my
car paid off … i made a bet with the almighty … when i got my car
paid off i would give my tips for one month to the homeless … i gave
a street newspaper seller a fifty dollar bill … he threw the papers
down and ran off … i guess to get high or drunk … i guess i was
enabling … i kept the deal … but after the car was paid off i was into
financial security … i felt secure in my life … so i quit … just up and
quit for no reason at all …

… after a week or two i became bored and decided to get another
hair cutting job … i went to the yellow pages and started to call barber
shops … i called one … the manager told me to come down and that
i would have to work for a week or two to see if i worked out … she
liked me but the owner of the shop could not stand hairdressers … it
was a great experience as i learned to barber … and that is a plus for
a hairdresser … i got so good i could cut four heads an hour … it was
an oldtime mens shop … guys would come in and say just give me a
regular haircut … i never did figure out what a regular haircut was but
they seemed to like what i did … i was rocking and rolling … i was a
cosmetologist among the barbers and was keeping up … the haircuts
were eight dollars and i took home five to seven hundred a week …

… cutting eight dollar haircuts …

… yeah … they all gave me ten bucks … all i had in expenses was
some products … talcum and the like … i even learned to shave with
a straight razor … on some saturdays i would make three hundred …
but there was a pall hanging over me …

… sounds dramatic …

… ah … but it was … i was working there illegally … the owner had
a barbering business license not a cosmetology license … and as time
dragged on he wanted me out of there … even though he made from
eight to eleven hundred in rent per month from me he was worried he

would get fined or have his license suspended … that would affect everyone in the shop … he started to make my life miserable … he could have just asked me to leave because of the situation but he was in his cups most of the time so what was i to do … after almost a year of barbering i walked in one morning and packed my stuff … i said two words to him over the phone and was gone … that was one job i did not want to quit …

    … was it because you were making so much money …

    … that and the fact that i was doing so well and had the respect of the other barbers … it was my life … i looked forward to going to the shop everyday …

    … were you still … i am sorry but this is funny … were you still going to drag shows …

    … oh yeah … i even got to go to some on the weekend … tell you a good story … this neighbor of mine in the apartment complex told me her niece was coming to visit with her boyfriend … she asked me if i could suggest any place for them to go … i suggested the desert museum … it is a real fun day out to see the wildlife of the desert … i told her i would be glad to take them … so off we went and had a fun day … it was on a thursday …

    … on the way back i asked them is they had ever seen a drag show … the boyfriend asked if the cars were on display … i told them i would pick them up at eight that evening … they had never been to see any drag and had a great time … you see … drag shows are good for you … i never went to one that was not a lot of laughs … i told the drag queens that they were first timers and they had a ball with them … the couple had an unforgettable evening …

    … allow me to digress for a moment … i have stated before that this treatise is written in the mind set i had at the time … it seemed perfectly sensible to do the things i was doing … even beating myself on the head to cast out the demons … i believed it would do me some good to do that … i kept it to myself … no one told me they noticed the bruises on the side of my head … then i made another big career move …

… i quit barbering yet again and decided to get into car sales … i joined a dealership and was set up for their training program … selling a car is like pulling teeth … i decided that i would not stand around the lot all day and wait for someone to show up … i tried to figure out a way to make cold calls to sell cars … i did not however want to bug people at home … so i came upon the idea of calling real estate brokers and agents … they were easily cataloged and filed for my call list … all i had to do was go on the net and pull up lists of agents by the company names … then i started to call … believe it or not i got some interest in my calls … i used the old technique of just telling them my name … that i was a car salesman and may i send them my card … it worked … i breezed through the classes and a part of it was to set up a sales plan with goals … i had about two months invested in this and with the few sales i had i figured i could sell six to seven cars a month starting out … the manager had a more compelling reason to set the figure higher … it was an unattainable goal and i knew i would fail … when i asked why the goal was set so high he told me he would not get a bonus if i sold less than the goal he laid out for me … huh … ah … what was i to do … well you can guess what i did …

… you quit …

… not only quit i decided it was time to go back to a a …

… you have got to be kidding … were you drinking …

… not at all …

… but you were getting desperate … i can sense it in your voice …

… indeed i was very desperate … i decided to take a few months off to figure things out … one of the things i figured out was why i kept going to a a … other than the wanting to belong to something …

… this ought to be good …

… i also started to go to a church … i figured between a a and church i would get straight …

… and hitting yourself on the head …

… oh absolutely … so off i went to a a and a real eye opener … the place i went was an a a hall … it was a couple of big rooms for twelve step meetings … with a room to sit around and drink coffee …

… going to that place was very intimidating … there were two or three guys and that is all they did was attend the meetings … they did not work … i do not know how they made money … anyway … these guys had all the answers to the sober life … i thought they were full of it … all they did was find fault with everything any of the others said … i noticed that people would start sharing stories that would meet with the approval of these guys … it was a a but to me it was a drunks codependents anonymous meeting … half the people there were still drugging and drinking as they had been sent there by the court …

… but the topper was the evening meetings presided over by this whacko with a rebel cap and a gravelly voice the people around the a a hall referred as the cowboy … he was mean spirited and would do nothing but put people down … he fed off the contempt he had for others … i of course was told i was useless by this character … i kept opening my mouth and he kept insulting me … it was the best thing that could have happened …

… anyway … everybody thought this guy was the answer to sobriety … he claimed to have twenty nine years without a drink … as i started to feel lower and lower about myself i also started to see some daylight … i may have been coming out of depression … really to tell you the truth i do not know what state i was in … mania … depression … both … it did not matter … then something happened that really got my attention … one night he came into the meeting after being gone a few days … now keep in mind this guy was the ultimate in sobriety according to the people there … so he comes in after being gone and sits at the end of the table not the usual spot in the center of things so he can pontificate … then i saw how full of it this guy was … i then noticed his features … drawn … shallow … pallid … he was a meth addict … this guy had not been sober for more than a week in his life …

… everyone bought into this fools line … i did not and it was an eye opener for me … at last i was figuring out why i kept going to twelve step meetings … they were making me feel bad about myself and it fed my very poor self image … i was not only beating up on my head … i was beating up on myself through these really disturbed people … twelve step meetings do not have healthy people in them … this was the biggest moment of clarity i had ever had … it was at that moment that i knew i had to get help … it had to be real this time as i knew i did not have many tries left … manic … desperate … depressed … no self worth … and attending a a for no reason at all … i did not belong to those people … i belonged to a better life … what a moment … what a new start …

… good for you …

… i did do the steps … but i wrote them for me … my first step was in keeping with the twelve steps jargon … i admitted i was powerless over bipolar disorder and my life had become unmanageable … i agreed that a power greater than myself could restore me to sanity … i went to the church to fulfill that step and step three which was i made a decision to turn my will and life over to the care of a higher power as i understood that higher power to be … the next two steps were easy as i was so down on myself …

… i made a searching and fearless moral inventory of myself … it turned out to be one hundred seventeen pages of typewritten truth as i could conjure it up … i was honest to a fault … i completed it about the same time i came out of my funk and into the light … i asked the minister at unity to hear my fifth step which was to admit to a higher power myself and to another human being the exact nature of my wrongs … he heard me out and then he told me i was ready for the sixth step that of having the higher power remove all my defects of character …

… doing these steps came at the same time i started to know i needed help and medication …

… sounds to me you did get something out of the a a meetings … tell me how many people in a a really do the steps …

… my impression … not many … but i am not the one to judge their program of recovery … i also found that as i gave myself a break i started to give others a break …

… another step i could add is not part of the twelve steps but i can say i came to believe that everyone else did not have to shape up for me to feel better …

... good for you ...
... so sal let us talk about the big break ... i have been straining at the bit to get into it and my big break in may two thousand four ... a month i will never forget ...

… enter doctor vicki …

… i saw myself walking down a lonely city street in the rain … the street glowed slick from the yellow street lights gleaming … i was hunched over with my trench coat drenched … my fedora poured a steady drip of rain down the front of my coat … i was a lonely man in a deserted city in the middle of the night …

… what was the theme music …

… jazz … with a sax blowing mellow …

… where were you headed …

… to an unknown destination … to the end of the street … and the street went on forever … it was a chilling experience … i just kept a slow pace …

… with the moment of clarity came less cycling … the thoughts were slowing down … it was the transition from the rage of mania to depression with a stop in between …

… the thirty five yard line …

… correct … but this time i knew better than to ride the wave and just enjoy the good feelings … i knew deep inside that i was headed for a crash and i wanted to stop that from happening …

… i got on the phone and started to call psychiatrists … for the first five calls i got an answering machine … i called the offices closest to me … i did not want to run all over town … then i hit the payoff … a real person answered the phone … she was the receptionist from doctor vicki …

. let me divert for a second … this is the part where real names will be used but they are restricted to my late wife judy my wife cathey my daughter denise doctor vicki and doctor stephen …first names only …

… so let me go on … the receptionist was very kind and tactful it inquiring about my health and mental health … i told her i had been diagnosed bipolar by four or five doctors … i told her i was on no medication and a little of the background about the inappropriate meds i had been subject to … i told her about my thirty five yard condition and that i did not know how long i would be in it … i asked for an appointment with as short of a wait as possible … she gave me an hour appointment two days out … at least i did not have to wait a week or two …

… when i wrote the appointment on my calendar i decided not to go anywhere or get diverted into anything else … i decided to stay in the apartment except for driving to her office to make sure i knew how to get there … and i went to the video store across the street and stocked up on sopranos episodes …

… it was still raining on my lonely street but i could see the end of it … i got a kick in my psyche just for making the appointment … i believed i would be well off after the appointment … i believed that i would not slip into depression or go up to mania in that short of time …

… *why the sopranos* …

… i had just started watching the series and was into the next season … i never saw the show when it came out … i do not like trying to follow story lines on weekly shows … you miss one and you are lost … i imagine i did not like my entertainment to be like that as my life was one missed episode after the other … yeah … that is a good way to put it …

… *no a a* …

… when i got a handle on my motive for going there and did those steps i had no need to go back there … why get into the mess if i no longer felt i needed to … it was part of the moment of clarity … let the cowboy scam someone else … i was also sure that with the help i was about to get i could learn to stay away from people toxic for me … i had not exercised very good judgment in my fellowships in the past …

… *what about the church* …

… i was still going there but i was only fooling myself … i was a jew for crying out loud … but i was teaching classes out of the old testament … i respected the idea of a savior but i never got used to the idea of eternal damnation … i could not figure that out … being forgiven or being tortured forever did not make sense … jews have no scriptures as to what will transpire upon death … i asked a rabbi what happens when a jew dies … his answer was how should i know … that is the way i feel about it …

… what about those conversations with god books … what is the theory there …

… good question … and theory is … how can anyone know … anyway the theory in those books is that you recycle when you die … you come back in another bodily form remembering nothing of the former life … so who can know if that is true … it posits a sensible outcome … one that pleases others … it is good to know that you do not know … tell me sal what do you think happens when you die …

… i think you just go away … the spirit may take on an ethereal form … maybe you are lucid and understand your past life …

… i think death is the ultimate moment of clarity …

… that is different … never heard that before …

… how did we get off on this …

… i think is was a question stored back there while you were talking about a higher power … what did you mean by a higher power …

… something greater than the psyche … something greater than myself and my powerlessness … it is like seeing into the future … listen to the news every night and you will hear someone predicting the future … this will happen if the government goes down this or that road … of course it never does … predicting the future is a guess … we are powerless over the future … our futures … and i believe the higher power is the entity that decides our future … now it stands to reason that if we do certain things our future can be predicted but not necessarily …

… example …

… okay … if you commit a crime jail may be in your future … but … do all criminals get caught … no … so therefore crime does not always lead to punishment … education is another … education does not always lead to success … having a bunch of degrees will not make you rich … i am a good case in point … between indiana and tucson i studied for an got a doctor of divinity degree from a seminary in new hampshire … so now i have two b a degrees … one masters … and a doctorate … what am i doing … cutting hair or unemployed …

… to tell you the truth i think you have done amazingly well … you provided for yourself in the face of some incredible odds … you are bipolar … that to me is a tough mental condition and you survived … through all that you had jobs that paid well and bettered your education … i think it is remarkable …

… well sal … now in my present mindset … my medicated mindset … so do i … it was a test of survival … i did it but it was a horrible struggle … i am very fortunate … i got an appointment with doctor vicki …

… oh yeah … i guess we can get back to that … so you watched videos for two days …

… and i was ready for the appointment … i had it all stocked up in my mind what i was going to say … i went up to her office an hour early and just sat in the car for about thirty minutes … i was just a ball of fire … i had very good vibes about this … up i went … i was at the end of the rainy lonely street …

… tell me all about it …

… i met the receptionist … she gave me a bunch of papers to fill out … they did not take my insurance but i could file that myself later … i just wanted the appointment … soon enough dr vicki came out of her office … i had confidence in her from the start … i knew she was an m d but i asked what was the discipline of her ph d … she told me bio chemistry … we sat and talked for about five minutes … i was prattling on and could not stop myself … in just five minutes she pulled out her script pad and wrote two prescriptions … we talked for the hour … i gave her my background and told her about my two failed marriages … she asked about any addictions to drugs and my alcohol use … i told her i never used drugs which was correct and then proceeded to tell her i had recently been attending a a … she again asked about my alcohol use and when i told her she asked why i was going to a a … i told her the two reasons … wanting to belong and poor self image … she told me to stop attending any twelve step groups and recommended a group for me … it was a bipolar group … since i was intimately familiar with the way groups worked i was very enthused …

… she asked about my employment … i told her i was taking some time off and explained my work record … she let me know that it was all right and that i should not beat myself up about it … doctor vicki was confident we were going to improve the work record in the future … she wanted to see me in a week … i was fired up about the new meds … with a bio chemistry ph d she had to have a handle on it … off i went with meds and a group to go to … and … best of all … a very understanding doctor …

… i felt i was leaving the thirty five yard line and going into a state of mania … i drove straight to the drug store which was right across the street from my apartment … i decided to allow the drugs to kick in and again not go anywhere … i started another season of the sopranos and had several books lined up to read … how soon would they kick in … indeed … how soon …

… and how long did it take for them to hit you …

… about three days … and on the one med i started at a real low dose and was to work up to a therapeutic level … but i could tell i was doing better as my mind slowed down … even though i was in the thirty five yard line range my mind raced … over the years i became adjusted to my mind churning and my mouth moving at a mile a minute … i do not think it is appropriate for me to list the drugs i was given as each bipolar has a different protocol of medication … i have yet to meet two bipolars with the same meds … most not even close …

… so you felt better after two or three days …

… after two days i felt as though the correct meds had been hit upon … i was both confident and enthused …

… did you not feel that way about the other meds …

… no not really … i never had confidence in the earlier medications … something about the prescribers … in this case i had all the confidence in the world about doctor vicki …

… this is the first time you have used names … any reason for that …

… i think it brings the ever increasing wellness into perspective … by that i mean i had developed good relationships … in the case of my daughter i redeveloped a relationship …

… why were you estranged from her …

… no i was just strange … and that brings another point up … i had … over the years … i had gotten into behavior patterns … i mean things like the drag shows and the church that i really did not believe in … and my sense of humor was way off … i would understand things my way and thought everyone else understood it that way … i knew i had to go through a big behavior change and that brings me back to my favorite book and favorite philosophy …

… in the absence of that which we are not that which we are is not …

… whoa … dude … you nailed that …

… i wrote it down and every once in awhile i read it over to remind myself of the concept …

so how did you use it with the changes in your behavior …

… i knew i would have to define or know the behavior that needed to be changed to be able to make the changes for the better … in the absence of the behavior that needed changing the behavior i needed to get to would not be there … i had to revisit the old behavior … in my head that is … i had to revisit it … i had to stop myself if i was acting nutzy and work through it …

… work through it …

… yeah … things like slowing my speech down … not trying to be the center of attention … not acting out even if it was by myself … and not beating myself on the head … that was a pretty easy one to stop … it was as if i had to get a grip on my emotional finances and not spend myself too recklessly …

… i think the first acting out i did was at the church i went to …

… the one you did not believe in …

… i think i was a little to harsh on the whole thing at that time … at least the minister did not preach hell and damnation … but getting back to it … i was to give a little invocation as the services closed out and i broke down … i started to cry for no reason at all … it was embarrassing and the minister got upset with me … i never went back … it was a matter of shame … it was like someone you know seeing you in a mental ward …

… being in a mental ward is nothing to be ashamed of …

… it was … when my former coworkers visited me in key west it was embarrassing … you bet … so here i was in front of the whole congregation crying … i believed it was a good thing as it taught me not to get in a maudlin situation and not want to be up front all the time … all things happen for a reason and that was a behavioral change …

… but you did not go back because you were ashamed … is that a good reason …

… oh i was ashamed for awhile but now as i look back on it … well it was a behavior that only happened once … but it was what it stood for … i considered it bad behavior and without that …

… you cannot know good behavior … good and bad being relative …

… you read my favorite book …

… i sure did …

… cool … anyway it was at that time that i was in the arizona corrections academy …

… you did not tell me about that …

… right after doctor vicki started me on the meds i applied to the arizona department of corrections to be a uniformed officer …

… after all your bad experiences with law enforcement agencies did you not think that was a bad idea …

… here is where a change of behavior came into play … in my former experiences i ended up in the middle of the problems of the supervisors that got convicted or fired … this time … knowing what i did about the system … i decided to stay out of the limelight …

however i did graduate number one … it was just my competitive attitude … but let me tell you about what i did before that …

… i went back east to a class reunion …

… but you quit high school … i take it was a high school reunion …

… yeah … it was the fortieth … and i decided to say hi to some people i had not seen in forty one years …

… how did it go …

… it was okay …

… just okay …

… yes … that was about all i could say about it … it was nice and okay … nothing to write home about if you catch my drift …

… why did you go …

… i had locked myself in that apartment for three years and needed to get out … so i decided to get way out …

… a change of behavior …

… indeed it was … and i made it a big change … it was all right that i was not a graduate … i was well received with the exception of one in the class … oh well … that was her problem …

… and that sounds like a big change of behavior …

… hey … you are really keeping up … indeed it was a change … not to get into psycho jargon but i … well … i let her own it … i am not responsible for any ones emotions or actions unless there is a love interest there … love is the melding of emotions … that to me is the definition of love … two emotions becoming one …

… i never thought of it that way …

… so letting her own her ill feelings toward me was a big step … before i would have treated the whole thing as if it was my fault … of having a fault because someone else is upset … how can i have a fault if someone does not consider me welcome at a reunion … that was hers not mine …

… that sounds like a big behavioral change …

… it was the start of the change … to this day i have to fight through that one … after fifty eight years of having been at fault ingrained in me it was a tough behavior to both recognize and change … i still fall back into it … not finding fault with myself got me away from the toxic drunks …

    … i take it you did not fall back into a a after beginning to work on your behavior changes …

    … why … that is what doctor vicki asked me … why was i going … the three years that i lived in the apartment i probably drank two bottles of wine and when i went out i always drank a non alcoholic beer … say with mexican food …

    … also i had by now changed my associations … i was with a bunch of cops and was through the academy …

    … by my count that was your fourth police academy …

    … i was getting pretty good at it by then … so i went in for my assignment and was assigned to a section of the prison that was almost all illegals on lockdown and we had one section that was hard lockdown … it was a part of the prison that was filled with real bad dudes … but they were locked down at night … and after a week of training on the day and swing shift i started on the deep nights shift …

    … the graveyard shift …

    … that is what they called it … in dallas we called it deep nights … it was a very smart move on my part … the pace was slow and i was with experienced officers … the deep nights shift had more time and experience than the other two shifts put together …

    … you wanted to stay out of the limelight …

    … i wanted no confrontations with the inmates … i just wanted to be there and do the admin duties … on the deep nights shift we checked out all the security devices and caught up on all the days paperwork … it was a good deal … we had twelve officers watching seven hundred sixty five inmates …

    … what …

    … yeah … but think about it … very little happened at night … i will tell you this … when it did happen it was something big …

    … for instance …

    … oh a suicide … someone cutting up … one inmate ate his broken television screen … had to med evac him … it was also a good way to learn spanish … i was so so with italian and did not have too much trouble with spanish … i took a course and got pretty good at conjugating verbs … i was doing real well …

… the benefit of working the night shift was that it was a four day work week … having three days off gave me a chance to work an extra day and build up comp time … i worked in another unit called minors … it was the facility for kids under eighteen that were convicted as adults … we had a few sixteen year old kids that were in for life no parole …

… good grief …

… they were very dangerous … they had to be handled by two officers … sometimes three … they were fed in their cells and were allowed out to go to school … you really had to watch them … again i worked the night shift and they were locked down … i also liked the reputation we had as night staff …

… the day shift thought that all we did was sleep at night … not so … and the swings shift could not understand why anyone would want to stay up all night in a prison … i enjoyed the staff and hours immensely …

… were you still living in your apartment …

… yes very little changed as to my living … i had a lot of socializing in the prison … but at home i was a loner … and i liked it that way … i mean i could reverse my schedule on my days off or i could just stay on schedule and stay up all night … i was glued to the tube a usual … i had two cats to keep me company and was making real good money … well the pay was not that great … twenty eight a year but with my retirement i had it very good …

… how about the environment … what about the bosses …

… on the night shift we had supervisors that were real good to work with … they wanted to be on that shift to get away from their supervisors … i worked on the weekend so i was around supervisors other than those on our shift for forty minutes in the evening and forty minutes in the morning monday and friday… and they were busy at end of shift and beginning of shift … every once in awhile they would even stoop so low as to talk to us … and i mean that … we were treated like vampires … that was the way i felt we were treated … and none of us had tans …

… by the time the holidays of oh four came around i was really settled into my meds … i had calmed down and a third med was added to really slow the cycling down and it worked … i had a great christmas with denise and her husband … she was seeing the biggest difference in me … and as the year closed out i was employed and had not had one thought of being found out or of quitting … and … in a state job … well you have job security … for the first time since the army i felt secure in a pay check …

… *what about layoffs and cut backs …*

… are you kidding me … we were at fifty percent strength … there was a period that we were forced into overtime because of lack of staff … that is endemic to law enforcement …

… *forced overtime … i guess you made some money …*

… nope … took it all as comp time … time off is better than extra pay … besides it just bumped up my taxes …

… *sounds like you were coasting right along …*

… things got better … along came judy …

… *ah … another name …*

... judy ... until death do us part ...

... after the holidays i decided to try online dating ... i got on a site and was amazed to find literally thousands of people on the site ... i put in my profile and added a photo ... it was an old photo and i felt it was a little deceiving but i put a blurb in the profile that the photo was a little out of date ... i met with three ladies and concluded that i was not right for them ... i did not tell them i was bipolar but did tell them i worked for the department of corrections ... i got the sense that they were looking for a lawyer or a doctor ... i had not the bucks to pursue any relationship ... i soon came to understanding that i may not be what anyone of the ladies on the site were seeking ... but i kept trying ... after a few weeks of looking at profiles i could read between the lines ... and then i met judy ann ... her profile was different ...

... how was that ...

... well she was not looking for something specific ... it was sort of open and her picture was well done ... she was an asian lady and i was soon to find out she was japanese from los angeles county and she moved here for her health ... she had pulmonary fibrosis ...

... she was on disability because of it ... before that she was a telephone techie ... i soon learned she was open to a meeting and we hit it off right away ...

... do you think you were prepared for a relationship ... you had been medicated for how long ... six months ...

... i may not have been ready but i had no idea i was not until i tried ...

... new behavior ...

… we really hit it off and decided to be exclusive … within four months we decided it was a good time for us to be together and i moved in to her place … she had a beautiful townhome but with her disability and pension she was on the edge with expenses … so my moving in helped … and we were together for awhile …

… awhile …

… yes … i had two mini meltdowns and she was trying to help me along … then the big meltdown came …

… what were the causes of the first two meltdowns …

… i was somewhat scatter brained as i wanted all of this to work out well and got into a mindset of not being good enough … i blew up twice and felt really bad …

… what triggered you to blow up …

… on several occasions judy found fault with me … plus my working the deep nights shift was putting a strain on us …

… so you felt not good enough …

… it was old behavior … old thought patterns …

… did you recognize it as that …

… i did after the fact … it was not as if i threw things around the house … it was just that i got angry and it was only for a couple of minutes … but i felt out of control and felt i had lost a lot of progress … judy talked me down and i think she felt bad for me … she recognized that we may have a bit of a struggle over my behavior changes … i was working on them and then the biggie happened … i blew up at one of her friends in a restaurant and walked nearly eight miles home … by the time i got home the friend was gone and needless to say judy was upset … i cannot blame her …

… what made you blow up in the first place …

… i thought the guy was being totally inappropriate by talking about his gay encounters in graphic detail … he was … well just to me … one of those guys that took advantage of everyone … i did not mind him as a houseguest but he kept up this gay love prattle and i got to the point i could not take it anymore …

… it was a big downfall for me and i called doctor vicki for help … she recognized my building anxiety and prescribed a fourth med … after about two weeks it helped me calm down …

… the tough part was that judy felt it was a good idea for me to move out as i needed to work on myself … but … even with that decision she was sticking by me … i moved into an apartment very close to work and we saw each other only during my days off … and before too long we were doing real well again …

… it was a good move as it taught me to guard my emotions better … plus the new meds really helped … my work was going along fine so i had the security of that … i did not like my apartment and i did not like the part of town i was living in … but i made the best of it … i watched a lot of videos and spent quite a bit of time on the phone with judy …

… then a guy at work wanted to sell an old trailer … he told me it was a fixer upper … i went to see it and figured i could work on it and make some money out of it … so i moved in there and got busy … i did everything … everything that is except the electrical … plumbing i can do … but wiring … i hired a guy to do that … i redid the living room and kitchen and painted the place inside and out … i put new flooring in and to make it a good deal i put all my furniture in it and made it a package deal … when all was said and done it took me four months of work … but i did a good job and felt it would go for a good price …

… you would not think the trailer … oh excuse me … you would not think a mobile home would go into the pits along with the housing market but it did … i sold it at a two thousand dollar loss … but before i put it up for sale i asked judy to marry me and she said yes … in the six months we had lived away from each other i was a completely different person …

… how was that …

… essentially i had calmed down … and my thoughts were my own …

… you were not cycling …

... not even when i was tired ... and judy noticed the change because she agreed to marry me ... we had not set a date ... one day while working on the mobile home i called her and said ... hey ... why do we not go down town and get a license and let the judge marry us ... she agreed and i was a very happy guy ...

... so the next day off we went to the courthouse ... they had a system as to coming in to get your license at three in the afternoon and then go to the courtroom at four ... judy was by this time wearing oxygen ... but we got all dressed up and got married on eight november of oh five ... we had been together for about a year and she had seen me through the worst of my turn around ...

... a week after we got married judy had to go in the hospital for two days for some tests related to her fibrosis ... a dense area was spotted on one of her lungs and just to be safe the doctors ordered a biopsy ... the next day the test came back positive for small cell lung cancer ... it had been twenty years since judy had a cigarette ... the doctors felt the fibrosis had weakened the lungs to allow the encroachment of the cancer ...

... we were devastated ... we knew that chemo was in the not too distant future ... we soon started a relationship with a chemo clinic ... it was a great facility ... the staff was superb ... judy was told that without chemo she would only live four months ... needless to say we opted for the treatment right away ... i had built up so much comp time that i went on short term disability for twelve weeks ... i was now a care giver and wanted to do the best i could ...

... we both knew that judy had little time left as small cell cancer is really the fourth and final stage of cancer ... judy decided to give the cancer a fight and took on the chemo with fortitude ... the first round was not the unpleasant sickening venture we thought it was going to be ... we had heard some horror stories ... into the chemo for about six weeks the tests came back that the cancer had spread to her organs and brain ... it was now time for radiation ... she braved that as well ...

... judy recovered from the effects of the chemo enough for us to take a week trip to cancun mexico ... it was good to get away from the house and have a little fun … she was feeling better and went without her oxygen … we went out to dinner … saw some shows … and had a good time … when we got back she was not as worn out as i thought she would be … we were encouraged by her bounce back … i was still on the deep nights shift as it gave me time to attend to judy during the day … she went to bed about the time i left for work …

… then the next round of chemo came up … this was the bout that gave her all sorts of grief … the sickness … the hair loss … the steroids puffing her up was all there … it was a very miserable experience and on top of it were the radiation treatments … judy was going through a round of poisoning … i do not know of any other way to put it …

… she was under the pall of the effects of the chemo for about three months … after that she recovered enough and got her strength back enough for her to go on a weekend trip to rocky point mexico … it was a three day outing and as with the last trip she recovered a bit … it had been fourteen months since the diagnosis … she had beat the prognosis by ten months … however … there is always a however … the cancer was spreading even more … it was building up in her system … more chemo in that short of time was too much for her … we had to delay it until the late spring …

… we became homebound as her breathing was becoming more dependent on oxygen … she often would remark that she knew she was dying … i was being strong for her … i did not let her down and during all of this we had an extra room built on the house … by this time we had refinanced to get the home in both our names … she wanted to expand the home and we did … anything for my judy …

… before she went into the third round of chemo we went to an outing in phoenix to see the beach boys and frankie valli … she was strong enough for the trip …

… the next week she started the third round and in fact all she did was start it … with the infusion of the first dose her vitals dropped off to practically nothing and her white count went to near zero … the nurses knew she would be bombarded with toxins … in effect the chemo was too much for her system … she was told by the doctor that she would not recover … she was told she was dying …

… judy was very brave and said to the nurses and me that it was time and that she had lived a good life … we had already selected a hospice and we called them … they had a bed open … an ambulance came for her … it overwhelmed me that she would never be home with me again … judy would never see her house with the new addition … a house she loved so very much … it was ours together … on the way to the hospice she drifted off and was only slightly aware of her surroundings … it was a very closed in room with a few pictures on the wall … i decided to bring some pictures from the house and put them up so it would be a little bit familiar for her …

… to my surprise the next morning when i woke up next to her she was awake and sitting up … i was going to stay with her and only leave to get a quick bite to eat and feed the animals … we had two cats and a dog …

… i stayed glued to judy in a lounge chair next to her … she was awake but tiring … for the first couple of days she drifted in and out … i called her mother and brother about her condition and they decided to come to tucson … they were there from the third to the sixth day she was in the hospice house … i stayed with her at night but the second night of his visit her brother stayed with her and for awhile she came out of her slumber and they talked … i was really happy for her brother and her mother that she was able to talk to them … when they left they knew it would only be a matter of days before judy would leave us … they both told me how happy they were that i was judys husband … during the hospice time i can say i never thought about my mental condition … i seemed to have it together and in retrospect i knew i was supporting judy the best i could … the night her mother and brother left she awakened and i told her a funny story about one of our cats … she laughed … she was in very good spirits … late that night or early morning she awakened and i told her i loved her and she told me she loved me … it was the last time we spoke … she nodded off into a semi coma … she was still feeling pain and the nurses would give her morphine …

… denise my daughter came on saturday morning to spend the day with us … early that afternoon my lieutenant from the prison came to visit and to see how i was doing … i was really impressed with that act of kindness … toward the early evening judy started labored breathing … i thought maybe the morphine was too much for her … blood had mottled around her joints and i knew then it was a matter of a very short time … judy drew three very labored breaths and died at eight that evening … she waited until she could be alone with me … denise went to feed the animals to leave me there … that was when judy decided to leave … just she and i in the room … i was quiet and her favorite c d was playing … somewhere over the rainbow … she was named after judy garland … my judy ann was gone …

… i went home about three in the morning after i had judys body conveyed to the funeral home for cremation … her wishes were to be cremated and to have her ashes spread over the desert … when i arrived home i found the house to be very empty … i told our boxer sammie and our two cats poppi and yuki that their mom was not coming home … of course they did not understand the language but they knew something had happened as their mom was always there with me and now in the middle of the morning i had arrived without judy …

… i sat quietly for awhile and cried for a bit and then i decided to celebrate judys life and not pine myself into fitful loneliness … i came out of the blues with that thought …

… that quickly … that first day …

… yes … i owed it to judy to stay positive and not fall back into a state of depression … we had worked too hard to get me between the thirty five yard lines and keep me there … i owed it to judy to stay mentally healthy … i was able to sleep for a few hours and then got up to a bright morning … that day i did nothing … oh i watched some t v and sat around the house … but i was not maudlin … my daughter came over to see how i was doing … i think she was surprised to see me so fit … in the head that is … we talked over the next few days and i expressed that i was going to give it a week or so before i started to

do all those administrative details incurred with the death of a spouse
…

    … i decided to hang on to very little as i believe that when someone
is gone it reduces your memory of them if you hang on to material
things … judy had a wooden box that she keep money and some other
valuables in … i decided that would be the memory box for my judy
…

    … i also decided to go back to work on that thursday … that gave
me from sunday through thursday to get my thoughts organized …

    … you did not sit shiva …

    … no … i actually thought about it … i am not that devout …
besides i always considered that focus was on the sitter and not the
loved one … i may have misinterpreted it but i knew i had to keep my
mind off if me …

    *… so what you are telling me is that you were not overwhelmed by
judys death …*

    … do you remember me telling you about judy talking about dying
… about us discussing dying … judy had planned for her death …

    … planned for her death …

    … yes … think about it … she knew she was dying and when the
chemo put her into an almost comatose state she knew it was time …
she went to her death with a brave heart … i think … because of all
the pain and the sickness from the second round of chemo … well …
i think she was relieved the end was near …

    … for the week she was in hospice she faded in and out of
consciousness … maybe she was going over to the other side … or
maybe she was shown the other side and had no fear …

    *… not to get off track … what do you think she saw on the other
side …*

    … whoa … that is impossible for me to answer … i think it gave
her peace …

    … how did you sense that … that she was at peace …

    … in her demeanor the few times she was awake …

    … do you ever wonder what is on the other side …

    … of course … and my opinion of death is as good as anyones …

... but what about all the experiences you hear about ...

... you mean near death experiences ...

... yes ... there are all sorts of books about it ...

... oh yeah ... i have read some of them ... halls of records ... golden cities ... meeting all of your family that preceded you in death ... all that ... but those impressions come from the imagination ... not death ...

... how can you say that ...

... death is life ceasing ... there is no more life ... all life has left the body never to return ... now with near death experiences the optimum word is ...

... near ...

... exactly ...

... so you give them no credit ...

... no ... because the people who experienced them were not dead ...

... you hear of people dying ... being clinically dead and then coming back to life ...

... clinically dead is not the definition of dead ... all life ceases ... obviously all life did not cease ... you know how to tell someone is dead ...

... how ...

... hold a mirror up to their nose and see if they are breathing and if you see no breath listen for a heartbeat ... you can have a heartbeat and not be breathing but you cannot be breathing without a heartbeat ... now ... i admit just by putting your ear against some ones chest you may miss a faint heartbeat ... but if they respond later with a greater degree of animation ... well they had not ceased all life ... how could they ...

... but all the experiences written about ...

... yep ... lots of books out there and they all tell people what they want to hear in one form or another ... it is like authors who claim to hear from the dead ...

... lots of books ...

… you bet there are lots books about seers and conjurers … one night i felt judy next to me in my sleep … i woke up … and guess what … judy was not there … the mind and dreams can come up with all kinds of experiences … but they are all in the imagination …

… imagination …

… how did we get off on this track …

… death is a fascinating subject …

… i came to fear death less after judy … i also believe there are those that do not fear death … although i have met a lot of people that thought they would not be killed …

… in the army … in vietnam …

… yeah … the folks that would stand up during a rocket or mortar attack … there is a psyche that goes with believing you will live forever … and not just the foolish … there is the case of the founder of unity church that wrote and truly believed he would live forever … all that changed at age eighty nine …

… but you were prepared for judys death …you knew she did not have long to live when she was diagnosed with small cell cancer … and she knew it too… let me see … let us get back to your returning to work …

… the second night i was home without judy i called my sergeant and let her know judy had died and i decided to come in for my regular shift that week … she felt it was too soon … but i told her how i was not going to languish in judys death … she understood …

… what about the administrative things you mentioned …

… oh … that was a matter of everything from accounts to insurance to social security to the mortgage and the deed … it all fell into place as we had planned for all of that … i had it all done in about three days … judy knew the importance of getting our affairs in order … we had refinanced the house together and had both our names on the car titles … it was just good planning … we did it for each other … i could have proceeded her in death … one never knows about such things …

… that does bring up a good point … one that i have to attend to … when you are single you do not think of such things …

… being prepared … well … it just takes the burden off of your survivors … also i decided to get all the memories down to that one box … i gave some of her clothes away to coworkers at the prison and the rest i took to goodwill … it was actually refreshing …

… now that is an odd word to use …

… not really … the good clothes went to ladies who would appreciate them and the everyday wear went to people in need … also there was the ring …

… the ring …

… judy had this huge diamond given her in another relationship and i did not want it … she talked about it several times … she decided to give it to the arizona lung association … and i fulfilled her wishes …

… may i ask …

… over seven thousand dollars …

… whoa …

… i also sent a lot of her jewelry and pottery to friends and her mother and brother … they appreciated that gesture … i think it was the second night i was alone when i called the gentleman from her former relationship … he appreciated the call also …

… so you just went on with work …

… yeah … work and exercise … i ran a lot after judy died … sammie would go with me … he was a big help to fill the empty house … i cannot tell you how much that boxer helped me … alone as we were … the big thing is … well … i stayed in good shape both psycho and soma … denise was a big help … she drove me to the funeral home to pick up judys ashes … that was a tacky experience …

… how so …

… the ashes were in a little cardboard box …

… you would have thought they at least would have put them in an urn …

… exactly … also … i was taken aback at how little ashes there were … the packet fit in my hands …

… so you were a bipolar guy that just lost your wife …

… and i did not go off the deep end …

… good …

… well not really …

… uh oh …

… not so much of an uh oh as a why did i do that … i allowed myself to be taken in by televangelists …

… get out of town …

… yeah … i could not get enough of it … i would watch them in the mornings before i went to bed and on my days off i would stay up all night and watch them … i sent away for some d v d s and books … i derived comfort from them … or at least i thought i did …

… thought you did … how so …

… after awhile i started to see through the whole scheme … a lot of what they had to say was on the same theme …

… and that was …

… if you give a lot of money away you will receive more … now that did not set too well with this old jew … and that was another thing … i was bound for the inferno if i did not give myself to their way of thinking … i stuck with it because in the beginning i thought i was getting something out of it … but after awhile … well … it was a scam for crying out loud … case in point …

… go ahead …

… the idea that if you give more money you will get more money … i happen to know that if you give a lot of money away you will have a lot less money … the other way defies economics … plus i had the experience of giving all my tips away that one month … you know … when i was working in the barber shop … whatever … and of course they wanted the money i was giving away to be sent to them … ah there was the rub … aside from the few books and d v ds i sent one of them thirty dollars … so i cannot feel ripped off … i started to … well … one day fooling around on the computer i started to look up some of the preachers … hum … one spent twenty three thousand dollars on a gold lined toilet … you have to think you are something special to have a gold potty … another hanged out with hookers and another with a male prostitute … a few were being investigated by the i r s …

… gives a whole new meaning to the golden throne … so you got over the fire and brimstone …

… yes … but …

… ah there is a but …

… but i was unhappy with myself for falling into the trap …but i keep coming back to being a nice jewish boy …

… but you said you were not devout …

… well … i guess … you know … i never liked scare tactics … my folks used that on me … if you do not do this or if you do that you will get a beating … sets in your psyche pretty well … and that is what all that hellfire and brimstone is to me … the psyche of the damned … who is anyone to tell you you are going to burn in some furnace beneath the crust of the earth for any number of reasons … and for eternity … my question is this … what would be the point … you are on the earth seventy years and you get punished until the ends of time … you must have done something really bad to deserve that …

… maybe being investigated by the i r s …

… exactly … what is heaven anyway … read genesis encryption … go ahead get it at the bookstore or order it online and you will understand … you will have a better understanding as to what the heavens are as mentioned in the old testament … but i am getting off track …

… i have got to ask this … did you tell doctor vicki about the evangelists …

… no and that was about the time i started to see through it all … if it was something i wanted to hide from doctor vicki it was probably not good for me … and it was not … i felt it set me back quite a bit …

… do you not think you are being a little hard on yourself …

… perhaps … but if i was not hard on myself i would not be where i am today … remember medication and behavior … they go together …

… so you got over the gold potty person … then what …

… it was getting on to the holidays … as luck would have it i was on a schedule that had me off on christmas day … and could spend it with denise and her husband …

... christmas ... you are jewish ...

... denise was not ... besides when in rome ...

... i get it ...

... then i decided to try to reach someone online ... just someone to get to know and be with ... i could not depend on denise for all my company ... so i returned to the dating website ... it was about the third day i was into it and a pop up came on ... it said introducing a new subscriber ... i took one look and said to myself ... do not goof this up ... and it was then that cathey entered my life and that my friend is a whole new chapter ...

... let us get started ...

... cathey ... bipolar passengers ...

... today i am hyper ...

... why ...

... because i am about to write the most important chapter of this book ...

... and how is that ...

... i think i am as good as i will get ...

... you mean bipolarly speaking ...

... bipolarly ... is that a word ...

... it must be i just said it and i am a newspaper reporter ...

... cool ... you know when i started to write this i had a different idea ...

... this chapter or the whole book ...

... the whole book ... i was going to do it verse by verse from ecclesiastes ...

... i do not know too much about that book of the bible ...

... it has to do with the futility of life ... that the end of it all arrives at nothing ...

... sounds depressing ...

... and that is the reason i did not continue with it ... i deleted over a hundred pages ... ecclesiastes repeats the same theme ... i thought it would be too much of a bummer for three hundred pages ... but i did get one very important message from it ... with all the doom and gloom i discovered that we ... bipolars ... we do not make our own gloom and we cannot get out of it either ...

... what about your behavior changes ...

… i could not have gotten to that without the medication … appropriate medication is the key to bipolar disorder … i believe there are those that are prescribed the proper meds yet do not work on the past … the past behavior … so the same things can crop up after the meds set in …

… such as …

… things like spending … not finding a steady job or going from job to job … and the big one is not taking responsibility… it is easy to fall back on the excuse of being bipolar and therefore i act the way i do … it is very much like alcoholics using the idea that they have an incurable disease and therefore act the way they do … you can always find an excuse … not to do that is to get well …

… get well …

… yep … meds first and then a life anew … and that is what i found online that evening when the new subscriber popped up … let me start at the beginning …

… please …

… i went on line to get to know someone … i was only on for three days and had not posted a picture yet … i told very little about myself in the profile … in the portion of the webpage that was mine there was a section to define what i was looking for … i merely put down that i cannot describe her but i will know her when i see her … i also put down that i was widowed and only wanted to date a widow …

… sort of narrowing the field were you not …

… think about it … who can know the feelings of a widowed soul better than a widowed soul …

… when the new subscriber came up on the screen did it say she was widowed …

… yes … in her profile it did … i sent her a response that was just a wink and she wrote back … we exchanged a few messages that evening … i was taken by her from the beginning … i knew something good had just happened to me …

. okay . i am going to kick back … tell me the story …

… after two days of email back and forth and me putting my picture on the site … well … we really pounded the messages out … back and forth for two days … the evening of the third day i sent cathey my phone number … my phone rang in about thirty seconds … we were both anxious … i did not want to say something stupid but i had to get it out … what i mean by that is i needed to tell her i was bipolar … i guess i got real dramatic about it … i have something to tell you i said … she probably thought i had outstanding felony warrants or something like that … i said to her … i am bipolar … she replied … i am bipolar also … took the wind right out of my drama …

… we had also written that we each had a dog and two cats … and that we had lost our spouses to lung cancer … and that we were with our late spouses when they died … we talked for three hours … we also decided to meet the next day … it was that meeting that did it for me …

… i had a lot spinning around in my head … not cycling … but no matter your age you revert to the high school mantra … what if she does not like me … kind of a crush manifesting itself in my bipolar being … i was very excited about the meeting … i had no intention to get involved in a deep relationship … which means i probably had an intention to just let things flow … who knows who is behind door number one … but i did not want to go to door number two or three … with cathey i stopped the search … not interested at all in meeting someone else …

… i got to the coffee shop first … i knew i would recognize her as i had her picture etched in my mind … i saw her approach outside the glass door … she was beautiful… i stood up as she came in as i did not want her to try to find me in the crowd … she saw me and came right over to the table … we stayed standing and i took her hands in mine and told her there was nothing to worry about … and to be calm … she was very nervous … i told her everything would be just fine … i was nervous but tried not to show it … our meeting was like our first phone call … it went on for about three hours … during that time i told cathey that i thought we were meant to be together as our late spouses got together on heaven dot com and wished us well … she thought it over for a bit and liked the idea … every now and then we go back to the memories of that first meeting and remember several things ... one ... cathey came dressed as she had been in her picture ... hat and all ... two ... she remembers me taking her hands in mine to calm her ... three ... the heaven dot com ... i had not thought of it until we met ... and we often use the ...everything will be just fine ... in our life together ...

... we agreed to be exclusive ... we both knew where the relationship was headed ... and we both knew that the excitement of the relationship could put us into a state of mania ... if we had to define our state of bipolar being it was very close to the top of the thirty five yard line ... we did not crest the line but were real close ...

... as i think of it now i have a very disoriented recollection of our first month together ... so in retrospect i was probably in the high of hypomania and just did not want to admit it at the time ... and we both knew cathey was in a state of mania by her activities ... we kind of bounced back and forth between our houses and my place was overrun with furniture ... we decided to give some away ... while i was working at night cathey would rearrange the rooms and each time she made the house look better and better ... she would come over before i went to work and would bring mybuddy over ... mybuddy is her dog ... he got along with my boxer real well and it was mybuddy that put me in the best standing with cathey ... she invited me over to her house ... mybuddy came right up to me ... that was unusual for him as he was afraid of men ... he may have been abused before cathey rescued him ... silly as it sounds ... that one event did more to cement the relationship than any other event ... i will forever be grateful to mybuddy ...

... i noticed cathey was getting more and more hyper as she got more and more industrious around my place ... she was not taking her meds which worried me ... i knew as manic as she was she was due for a crash ... we had gotten together during the holidays and people are generally up emotionally anyway ... with bipolar it is even more so ... it was about the end of january oh eight that cathey had a downturn ... she stayed at her place for a few days ... mostly in bed ... i convinced her to get back on her meds and to please stay on them

… you know … after that day she has been very good about her meds …

… back to the house situation … i moved into catheys place in late february … things were moving fast … digressing a bit let me tell you about her parents … i met them about a week or so after we met … they were charming … they lived in a very upscale retirement village … i had learned that catheys mother was sicilian … when i met her i called her by her maiden name … i could not have started the relationship off on a better foot … her father was very polite to me but was a little worried for his daughter … that was to be expected …

… we seemed to move very fast … me moving in and all … but that was okay … we did not owe an explanation to anyone … catheys neighbors were very kind to me but i could see … they too … were concerned for cathey … i decided to guard my behavior as i had never done before … no manic outbursts and not too much of my whacko sense of humor … however … i did … on our first date … take cathey to a drag show … it was not the usual … it was vegas top drawer … she liked the silliness of it all … that would be the last drag show i would see … again a change in behavior …

… one thing kept cropping up in my head … what was i going to do with the house … my house … i was not living in it anymore … at catheys place we now had four cats and two dogs … and i had a house full of furniture in a very depressed market …

… here i am going from market to marriage … when i asked cathey to marry me i had confidence she would say yes … she did … also we decided to get married in the next county … we did not want to announce it to the world or at least to the folks in tucson … we got married on eighteen april oh eight … we told her parents and our neighbors … i was not manic and i was happy beyond explanation … i had met and married the most wonderful person in my world … cathey is a delight … i cannot express how proud i was to have cathey as my wife … a meeting of the minds is one thing but a meeting of bipolars was fabulous … to outsiders it probably seemed like a wild idea … but medicated bipolars are able to help each other through the tops and bottoms and we are able to do that … when we told her dad he was very pleased … her parents probably did not like us living together … if they would have known what we were doing with catheys money they would have had a fit …

… let us go to that … i took my money out of the market when it was … the dow that is … when the dow was at fourteen thousand … cathey was losing a lot of money from this facocta broker … he had her in all stocks and the account was bleeding … we talked it over and cathey … on my recommendation … decided to move her money to a discount firm and manage it herself … also at my recommendation … now this is before we got married … so cathey was placing a lot of trust in me … she moved the account to a discount house and started to sell out the stocks … they were headed south and when it was all over she got out when the market was around twelve five hundred … i am telling this story to give you an idea of how much cathey was willing to rely on me … it was not that i was a broker in the past … that has nothing to do with good money decisions … i do not make money decisions on analysis … i make it on gut feeling and i recommended to cathey that she get out of all her stocks … it was a gut reaction and a good reaction … the market … the dow … went down to sixty five hundred … she got out and kept most of her earnings … and through the whole affair we worked together on it … she did so well for her financial future … enough of that … let us get to the real bugaboo in our first few months of being together … my house …

… after a thorough sprucing up directed by cathey who staged houses for a real estate broker … i knew what i had to do … i followed her instructions to the letter … i was in a down period while all this was going on … we decided that the furniture was best sold with the house along with all the appliances … everything else went … truck load by truck load … to goodwill … the house was beautiful and ready for sale … it was the calm before the storm … now comes the home inspector … lord … one thing after another … it was the first of my manic fit flips since we were married … new roof to begin with and a bunch of other things that i could fix … i just needed the time and materials … i over reacted to the inspection … the real estate broker told me it was nothing … that the inspection went well … i thought it was horrible and stated so in the garage pacing around in circles … cathey and the broker got me calmed down … and when i got to the fix ups it was really not that bad … the inspection was conducted because we got an offer for the house … i got a new roof and the rest of the work done … the buyer moved in on a lease to purchase agreement … katy bar the door … lesson learned …

… while all of this was going on we got married again with a preacher and family and friends … it was a grand affair … cathey was beautiful … she is always beautiful … and i had my dress blues on … the ceremony … the pictures … the whole day was a success … i did not let the house bother me that day … it was the eighteenth of july oh eight … it was a wise decision to get married with a ceremony … we were attending a church for awhile and the minister was kind enough to come to the banquet room to marry us … this was to be our last church experience … we left the church shortly thereafter … the best way to describe the experience is that the services left us unfulfilled …

… spiritually we moved together on our own … i introduced cathey to the book conversations with god and she fell in love with it … we had study nights with the book and a study guide … i know i keep going back to conversations with god … it is worth the time to get to know …

… the house was to be the best thing that ever happened to us … at least happened to me to make us stronger … the lease was a disaster … i forget how it came about but there was a spot of mold found behind the sink in the kitchen … it was a spot the size of a dollar bill … i am grateful to the insurance company … they paid the repair … three grand … and then the leasee decided she did not want to buy the house and left it in a mess … seven thousand dollars in damage … again the insurers came through … and she had taken all the furniture … so i used the insurance money to completely redo the house and then cathey staged it … it was during the transition period that what happened is now known as the red truck incident … we were sitting in my red truck outside of a bookstore and the pressure of the house got to me … i went into a deep manic rage about having the house on my back … it scared cathey and she was very upset … she told me that she was afraid the marriage was not working out … i was terrified and remorseful that i had caused those feelings in cathey … it was an event that was to give me the most radical change in my behavior that i had ever undergone … i realized right then and there i would have to rid myself of the demon of mania … i had hurt my cathey and for several days i hated myself … it was not a matter of her believing i would change … it was a matter of my proving it to her and i was bound and determined to do that …

… after the red truck incident i still had concerns about the house … but things got better … cathey staged the house to look its best … it was grand … the first person to walk in bought it …

… we were elated over that development … but the down side was that we gave the house away to sell it in a very tough market … all told i lost twelve thousand on the home but i had the equity to break about even … zero sum gain …

… by the summer of oh eight i was on terminal leave with the department of corrections … i was pleased that my bipolar self made it for four years and that i did not leave in a huff … i resigned and said my goodbyes like a gentleman … i was on my best behavior …

… by this time i was working part time in a salon … it was the same company i had worked for before … denise thought i was crazy to do that … i told her it would be all right and that i was a different person … the shop was only five minutes away and being part time cathey and i had a lot of free time …

… i first want to discuss my family … because of the meds i could get to the level of being part of a family … when we had the red truck incident that sense of family was threatened and i was determined to correct myself and stop acting out over stress … i was not worried about joining a group or saving the world … my meds gave me a good sense of self and i wanted to do well for our family of two … and six animals …

… cathey and i spent our time together as both lovers and friends … we knew that self and family is about all the responsibility we can take being bipolar … to get off track away from self and family will throw us off and have us playing outside the thirty five yard line … it is unsafe for us mentally to venture into group dynamics … self and family only …

… any step beyond those two levels of being could be a trap … we decided to do a lot of things together and one of them was to write … cathey had the idea that the writings i had done could be good book material … i had a manuscript of a story of a wise guy … i called the book … canzio … a sal luca gig …

… thank you …

… ah … good … you have joined me … after that title we decided that all of our books would be sal luca gigs … we even gave you a little background … we brought you to life so to say … we got a publish on demand company to do the books … you can spend years trying to find a publisher … a commercial publisher that is … so we went with a publish on demand deal …not until the books are ordered are they printed … but we got a two for one deal …

… i had written … let me start over … for the last fourteen years i have written a short story with a holiday theme every christmas … the stories have a twist for an ending … cathey thought the stories would make a good book so we set about editing the stories and all but one the ending was changed and enhanced by cathey … the title is… santa is out there … christmas tales from the edge … a sal luca gig … and i have to tell you that the cover designs for both of those books were created by cathey and they are excellent …real works of art … she is so very talented …

… well we got those published … we were looking for a commercial publisher for our third book … we came across publishamerica …

… the book was from genesis … the first ten chapters … verse by verse with explanations by an angel interviewed by … who else … sal luca …

… i remember that …

… it was called … genesis encryption … a sal luca gig … six angels are interviewed … i wrote and cathey edited … it was exciting for both of us … and catheys artwork became the cover as well … we had rewarding experiences writing together … and we continue with this book ... again by publishamerica ... cathey and i got rave kirkus reviews for the christmas stories ...

... congratulations ...

... sal i love to talk to myself through you ...

... where were we ...

... oh yeah ... back to the story of cathey and family ... a lot came together that fall of oh eight ... the house closed ... i left the department of corrections and i was working part time at the shop ...

... cathey was not to crazy about me working in the shop ... it was not good for me ... and i was not happy there ... i got through the holidays of oh eight and into the new year ... i sat down and put a pencil to the wages i was making and the amount of social security i would make and it turned out i was working for about three hundred dollars a month ... it was enough to get my attention ... and as soon as my manager quit under stress i quit ... i left a professional letter of resignation and was ... on that day ... fully retired ... it took me about ten minutes to get used to it ...

... really ...

... yes really ...

... i hear so much about retirees getting stressed at not having anything to do ...

... cathey and i found something to do ... we volunteered as citizen officers with the oro valley police department ... we even went through the citizens academy ... it was fun at first ... but we were venturing into the third level ... the group dynamic ... we had to guard against interrupting the self and family ... it is not important to the story as to what we did ... what was important is that at the same time we both agreed that it was not healthy for us to continue as we had just started this book ... we were both stressed by it ... retirement for us is just that ... lack of stress ... we have learned that we do not have to be doing something to have a good sense of self ...

... sounds healthy ...

... it is for us ... cathey and i have a no conflict understanding ... we have no conflict and look for no conflict ... really ... we have no conflict with each other ... we are now involved in a mini group dynamic … we each do things for the home owners association … cathey is very busy … on the computer with being the treasurer … but it is administrative and not a group effort … i do the irrigation management … it means turning on a few valves … alone … no group dynamic … dealing with some of the residents can be exasperating … but we handle it well and i have learned not to over react … cathey has taught me the principles of non conflict …

… oh boy … what is that …

… really … what is worth a big quarrel … just let it go … it takes the ego out of it … and the more you practice it the easier it is …

… but life is conflict every day …

… ah … not really … not for us … we do not have jobs … we have no conflict between ourselves and we avoid conflict with others … it is restful and sane … it is sort of the practice of diplomacy on the personal level … besides it is fun to let the complainers win …

… complainers complain to win do they not …

… not really … the psyche of the complainer is to raise a stink about anything … they are always looking for a fight … ninety eight percent of complaints in something like the home owners association come for two percent of the people …

… i agree with that …

… so in comes the guy complaining about his bushes not getting enough water … so i just tell him i will water his bush more … i do not argue with him and he will move on looking for a fight … i can tell what they are going to say before they say it … and it is all caused by cable news stations …

… huh …

… i know this first hand …

… this ought to be good …

… it drove cathey crazy … i used to be a real news junkie …

… i can understand that … many retirees are … did it affect you that much …

… it affected cathey very much … she could see me setting myself for a possible slip into mania as i became upset with the pundits on the cable news shows … i would watch hour upon hour of news …

one hour segments on top of the other … they all lead with the same stories … it was the same stuff over and over and i would get drawn into the drama …

… cathey said very little and she knew i had to find out for myself … a few times we talked about it and her concern as to how it affected me day in and day out … and then one day i realized that it all had to stop … it was doing me no good … so i just quit watching the stuff … i just quit getting myself excited over nothing … the longer i stayed away from it the better i got … i was months away from the news when we decided to watch some election results in oh ten … i could not stand it … it was all a waste of time … i could read about it the next morning in the paper and it would take me about five minutes …

… the point i am trying to make is that one can get immersed in events that one has no control over … get angry with actions of others that are far removed from ones reality … big deal …

… big deal what …

… big deal if someone in mississippi finds fault with the president … big deal about the chatter of the speaker of the house … i really do not care and if it had not been for catheys gentle guidance i would still be watching and kvetching at all those events that seem to foment hostility in so many people …

… kind of hard on the news business are we not …

… i am not talking about the news business … that is a half hour every week night … i guess the news only happens monday through friday … anyway … what i am talking about is how the pundit shows create anger and contempt in people … i bet you that all the people that complain all the time about everything … i will bet you they watch cable news pundits long into the night … it is not what others do that is important but how it affects me and my bipolar …

… avoiding conflict …

… yes … and it is important for bipolars to do that … avoiding conflict or better stated … not starting conflict is probably the most important personality trait a bipolar can develop … this is not about the news and the experts and the pundits … it is about being mentally healthy …

... with that definition ... a lot of folks are not very healthy in the head ...

... hello ...

... so you credit cathey with your progress ...

... over the last three years and as of the writing of this book i can tell you i would not be where i am today ... would not be this healthy if cathey was not my wife ... bipolar to bipolar we understand each other ...

... let me ask this ... did you ever help cathey ...

... oh yes ... i think i helped her the most by getting her in the habit of taking her medication on time every day ... for both of us ... well that is the most important ... i can tell catheys moods ... well not moods ... call it her state of mind in her illness ... she missed her highs of not taking her meds and suffers lows in the extreme sometimes ... catheys depression is much deeper than mine ... sometimes she dips below the thirty five yard line ... and i tell her that it is okay ... not to worry and that she will come out of it ...

... putting it all together ... our conditions ... our bipolar ... i was easy to medicate compared to cathey ... where she is now in oh eleven is a lot better than when we met after she stabilized on meds ... she went through a long period of depression and near depression ... she seemed not to be able to get out of it ... her meds were being changed often and nothing seemed to work ... some of the meds made her sluggish and some made her anxious ... but she never quit ... now she has a very good match of meds and is doing very well ... it took awhile ... no ... it took a long time but she kept trying and trying ... i am very proud of her ...

... we both went through a long period of no or inappropriate medications ... and then got on track but it took awhile ... if i had but one message in this book it would be if you are bipolar you need medication and do not give up ... i do not mean to sound depressing but it may take a long stretch ... stay with it ...

... good advice ...

... cathey is my love ... we work together and edit each other ... she edits the books and i help her with her art and graphics ... we edit each others illness … it is a symbiotic relationship and i have become a confident and secure man with cathey in my life …

    … cathey has given me a life between the thirty five yard lines and i have done the same for her … what more could love be … we are bipolar you know …

    … i know …

Would you like to see your manuscript become a book?

If you are interested in becoming a PublishAmerica author, please submit your manuscript for possible publication to us at:

acquisitions@publishamerica.com

You may also mail in your manuscript to:

PublishAmerica
PO Box 151
Frederick, MD 21705

www.publishamerica.com

Breinigsville, PA USA
14 April 2011
259800BV00002B/4/P